THE PRIVAT

D1148131

LOCATIONS
series editors: *Stephen Barber and Barry Curtis*

LOCATIONS is a series of thematic books examining contemporary genres and hybrids in national and international cinema. Each book contains numerous black and white images and a fresh critical exploration of aspects of film's relationship with other media, major themes within film, or different aspects of national film cultures.

on release:
Animals in Film
JONATHAN BURT

Childhood and Cinema
VICKY LEBEAU

Dark Places: The Haunted house in Film
BARRY CURTIS

'Injuns!': Native Americans in the Movies
EDWARD BUSCOMBE

Projected Cities
STEPHEN BARBER

War and Film
JAMES CHAPMAN

Women, Islam and Cinema
GÖNÜL DÖNMEZ-COLIN

The Private Eye
Detectives in the Movies

BRAN NICOL

REAKTION BOOKS

To 'my' Patricia

Published by
Reaktion Books Ltd
33 Great Sutton Street
London EC1V 0DX, UK
www.reaktionbooks.co.uk

First published 2013

Printed and bound in Great Britain by Bell & Bain, Glasgow

British Library Cataloguing in Publication Data
Nicol, Bran, 1969–
  The private eye : detectives in the movies. — (Locations)
  1. Detective and mystery films—History and criticism.
  I. Title II. Series
  791.4'36556-dc23

ISBN 978 1 78023 102 0

Contents

Detective Charles McGrath in *The Narrow Margin*.

Introduction

'My name is Philip Marlowe. I'm a private investigator. I'm not
with the City, the County, the State, or the Feds. I'm not with any
collection agency.' *Farewell, My Lovely* (1975)

The private eye is one of the most instantly recognizable figures
in popular culture. Dressed in a suit and shabby overcoat, a fedora
on his head, a cigarette or a gun in his hand, he traverses the
labyrinthine spaces of the modern urban world. He is wisecracking,
hard-drinking, womanizing, disrespectful towards authority, as
capable of meting out violence as he is prone to receiving it.
The private eye is a 'lone wolf', who maintains few lasting relationships with women, keeps fewer close friends, and has only two
places he can call his own: a soulless apartment, and a sparsely
furnished office. His office is his more natural habitat, and from
there he is despatched to fulfil the demands of his endless, all-
consuming work.

Because of his fearless, solitary credentials, the private eye is
often thought of as a hero, a lone protagonist in an unforgiving
world. This is a trope central to American culture, which can be
found in the Western or in 'river-journey' narratives such as *Adventures
of Huckleberry Finn* (1884) or *Apocalypse Now* (1979). Raymond
Chandler, the creator of the private detective Philip Marlowe, and
the writer who, more than any other, influenced how the private

Humphrey Bogart as Philip Marlowe in *The Big Sleep*.

eye would appear on screen, famously said of the private detective: 'He is the hero, he is everything.' Chandler described him as the man who goes down the 'mean streets' of the modern city without being mean himself, and is 'neither tarnished nor afraid . . . , a man of honor, by instinct, by inevitability, without thought of it, and certainly without saying it'.[1]

Others have called the private eye 'the perfect existential hero . . . our surrogate, bold as we are cautious', a man who has 'reason to poke his nose into and to overhear the gossip from all strata of society on our behalf',[2] a man full of 'single-minded determination' whom 'you can punch down over and over again, but he'll just keep getting up and walking towards his goal',[3] and 'a pretty unbeatable archetype of modern masculine heroism: more independent than a policeman or a soldier, sexier than a Spencer Tracy priest, more virile than a screwball-comedy playboy and exponentially wittier than a cowboy'.[4]

Closer inspection of the films he appears in, however, reveals him as a man who is frequently the object of scorn or ridicule, often loses fights, and is repeatedly unlucky in love. The private eye faces a level of contempt rare among the heroes of popular fiction (think of the spy, in contrast). As much as he represents a form of idealized masculinity, and stands as a fearless, relentless exposer of corruption, he is also denigrated for being a peeper, a snooper, and – worst of all – an irrelevance. In the film *Harper* (1966), for example, the private eye is summed up as being 'hired by a bitch to find scum'. In *The Long Goodbye* (1973) Philip Marlowe is told to 'Go back to your gumshoes and your peeping and let us alone'. In *Chinatown* (1974) Jake Gittes is confronted by a disgusted man who has seen his picture in the newspaper and tells him, 'You got a hell of a way to make a living!'

Where Gittes is indignant in response, most movie private eyes accept that their lives are a long way from being heroic. An

Robert Mitchum as Jeff Bailey in *Out of the Past.*

earlier Marlowe, in *Murder, My Sweet* (1944), describes himself as 'just a small businessman in a very messy business', while Jeff Bailey, the private eye in *Out of the Past* (1947), begins his story with these words: 'I opened an office in San Francisco. A cheap little rat hole that suited the work I did. Shabby jobs for who'd ever hire me. It was the bottom of the barrel, and I scraped it, but I didn't care. I had her.'

We might also expect that movies revolving around a lone masculine hero would have suitably epic plots, much as the spy movie envelops its hero in the entanglements of international political intrigue. But when we examine the plots of private eye movies, they hinge on domestic or personal drama, caused by troubled family histories (such as *The Big Sleep*, *Harper* or *Chinatown*) or friends letting one down (*The Long Goodbye*). The 'métier' of the private detective, as Jake Gittes puts it, is 'matrimonial work'. One of the ironies about the hypermasculine Mike Hammer, the *Übermensch* version of the private eye who features in the film *Kiss Me Deadly* (1955), is that he specializes in

Mike Hammer mocked by the police in *Kiss Me Deadly*.

divorce cases. As the cops who interrogate him contemptuously reveal, this boils down to a kind of blackmail. One of them describes him as a 'bedroom dick', while another explains that 'he gets information against the wife. Then he makes a deal with the wife to get evidence against the husband, thus playing both ends against the middle.' 'Just how do you achieve all this?', they ask him. 'You crawl under beds?'

The word 'private' in the label 'private eye' is, in this respect, perfectly accurate. The private eye deals with *private* matters – and for private here we might read 'domestic', 'personal', or 'small-scale', the opposite of grand, public or professional affairs. It is true that private eye movies are thrillers and need to be exciting and full of suspense. Their plots typically show how the apparently mundane tasks which amount to the private eye's 'day job' – especially the staple of the tradition, the missing-person case – accidentally lead him to become embroiled in a conspiracy of a much wider significance and danger. Yet the private eye's concern with the domestic and the private spheres is more than just a red herring, a pretext for the movie's real interest in weightier topics. It is one of the most important, if submerged, obsessions of the private eye film.

This is what this book is about. Writers and critics, drawn to the symbolic connotations of the term 'private eye', have been most attracted by its second word, the 'eye'. Thus we have the detective as private '*I*', the independent, free individual engaged in an existential quest, or as private '*eye*', the man who looks boldly at things most of us would not dare to. While these symbolic interpretations are relevant to this book – especially the idea of what the private eye sees – it will pay more attention to the connotations of the first word, how private-eye films concern themselves with the *private*, than have previous studies of hard-boiled detective fiction and film.

How is the private realm – that is, private spaces, private lives, hidden selves – portrayed in private eye films? What impact does this have on the private eye himself, and on the viewer? There may well be something heroic in the task of unlocking private spaces – especially when we consider the curious paradox at the heart of many private eye films, that the detective's exploration of the private lives of others means sacrificing his own – but this element of detective cinema is of a different order to the intrigue and excitement of the thriller plot.

Private Business

Most obviously, the word 'private' in 'private investigator' refers to the figure's independent professional status. The value of the private detective to his client is precisely that he is not affiliated to the authorities. This is how yet another Marlowe (in *Farewell, My Lovely*) persuades a woman to let him into her apartment, by insisting that he is not working for any official body or private company. Even though the private eye may embody 'a principle of law which is superior to that signified by the police force and the legal system',[5] the prime objective of his cases is protecting the private interests of individuals rather than upholding statutory law.

Private investigation is a real-life business – albeit one far removed from its portrayal in cinema. It is easy to hire private detectives if you have the money, as even the briefest of Google searches will reveal. The real-life private investigator (like his fictional counterpart, as he is depicted before he becomes enmeshed in the film's plot) is likely to specialize in surveillance in order to meet the needs of suspicious partners, employers, and insurance companies – or even media organizations (as the recent UK *News of the World* scandal and the subsequent 2011–12 Leveson Inquiry

A trio of Marlowes: Dick Powell in *Murder, My Sweet*.

Robert Mitchum in *Farewell, My Lovely*.

Elliott Gould in *The Long Goodbye*.

into unlawful information-gathering practices revealed).[6] The private detective remains professional yet not public in the way that police detectives or government agents are. He is not employed by the taxpayer, but employed privately. Like a private company, his responsibility is therefore to his paymaster rather than any general notion of public good.

Private detection concerns itself with private activity, business that is either not in the interest of the wider public (in other words, it neither threatens them nor is likely to arouse their curiosity) or is the sort of thing clients specifically want to keep out of the public eye. Helen Grayle makes it clear in *Murder, My Sweet*, when engaging Marlowe, that his task to recover a valuable missing necklace (one of those simple tasks common in private-eye films that inevitably unravels into a complex and deadly drama) is to be performed 'without any publicity' because her husband has 'a morbid fear' of it. A similar scene occurs in *Harper*: the detective asks his seductive client, Mrs Sampson, who has summoned him because her husband has disappeared, if she has considered going to the Missing Persons bureau. She replies, 'Well, that might mean publicity. Ralph loathes publicity.'

Publicity is usually shunned, too, by the private investigator himself. In *The Long Goodbye* Marlowe regrets having his picture appear in the paper because it's 'bad for business'. Business, the mechanics of securing work and performing it well for payment – enough to ensure the business survives – is of paramount importance to the private eye. This is another definitive feature of the private eye movie which has often been overlooked. His work means that he runs a small business, and is self-employed. If successful enough he takes on staff. He therefore needs to preserve his economic independence at all times. Private eyes in the movies are always 'blue collar', needing to work to maintain a decent standard of living (like Mike Hammer or John Shaft in *Shaft*) or even just to survive (like Bailey in *Out of the Past*) – a far cry from a 'gentleman' detective like Conan Doyle's Sherlock Holmes, who has no apparent need to work to keep himself solvent. This realism about what it really means to work 'privately', to be entirely responsible for one's income, invites a sober readjustment of the conception of the private eye as heroic.

The private eye's status as an independent businessman, servicing the needs of private paymasters, leads to a dilemma about his ethical position. Writing about Dashiell Hammett's darkly pragmatic detective, the 'Continental Op', the critic Steven Marcus was struck by his 'moral ambiguity': 'Which side was he on? Was he on any side apart from his own? And which or what side was that?'[7] The private detective's keen powers of observation, his determination to combat criminality, and his freedom from the codes and policies of any organization, mean that he can figure as someone to be trusted, a do-gooder, even perhaps – as in *The Long Goodbye* – a 'good neighbour'. But, as others have pointed out, the private eye's morality can be ambivalent or even negligible.

In Joseph Conrad's 1907 novel *The Secret Agent*, the private detective is listed alongside 'keepers of gambling hells and disorderly houses' and 'drink sellers' as those who possess an 'air of moral nihilism'.[8] The private eye's proximity to the crime and his knowledge about who is responsible mean that, if so inclined, he can be in the perfect position to cover up evidence or manipulate the players in the drama for his own personal gain. In *Blood Simple* (1984), when private investigator Loren Visser is told by his client, Julian Marty, that he has a proposition for him, he replies: 'if the pay's right, and it's legal, I'll do it.' But when informed that what is on offer is illegal, he amends this to, 'if the pay's right, I'll do it.' He then kills the client and tries to frame the man's wife for his murder so he can claim the money for himself.

Jeff Bailey (Robert Mitchum) looking in on Leonard Eel's apartment in *Out of the Past*.

As well as being an investigator who is not publicly accountable, the private eye is an investigator of the private, that realm of existence which is visible only to the gaze of a select few or to no-one else at all. The private eye sees what other people don't – or sees what they *do* see, but in a different light. He looks into people's private spaces, parts of life not usually scrutinized by the state and its police until it is too late, and a crime has occurred. He examines their property, their private business, their private histories. He pries into peoples' sex lives (as Marlowe does when untangling the connection between Carmen Sternwood and the pornographer Geiger in *The Big Sleep*), and witnesses the most personal moment of all, their death.

The private eye's job is to scrutinize and present for our judgement the private lives of others, the aspects of their existence they prefer to keep secret. This function has particular consequences for how we think of gender in crime movies. Examining the way the private eye can intrude into *feminine* spaces (the subject of chapter Four) complements and complicates previous analyses by film critics about the charged sexual politics in film noir.[9]

The private eye movie is a variety of crime thriller, but as much as the films dealt with in this book are 'about' crime, they are also about an aspect of human nature which is broader and more mysterious than criminality: our *private* behaviour, desires and transgressions. Their plots are ultimately about 'private business', about things people wish to keep from the public gaze. This means secret crimes and unacceptable desires, of course, but also dysfunctional families, failing marriages, even a secret yearning for domestic harmony. Even those movies which are ostensibly about public scandal eventually turn out to be about domestic crisis; bound up with the political conspiracy in *Chinatown*, for example, is a horrifying personal and familial trangression.

Locations: The Scope of this Book

The private detective is a fixture in early twentieth-century literature, not just in u.s. 'pulp' fiction of the 1920s and '30s (which we shall consider further in chapter One) but in literary fiction by authors such as Joseph Conrad or Graham Greene. As a real-life profession, private investigation dates further back, to the French criminal-turned-official-investigator Eugène François Vidocq in 1833, and the first private investigation agency, Pinkerton's, in New York in 1850. Yet there can be no doubt that the private eye owes his cultural significance to the movies.

The history of the private eye movie roughly parallels the entire history of cinema, from Michael Curtiz's *Private Detective 62* (1933) to Tony Krantz's *The Big Bang* (2011). Yet there are two distinct 'moments' in which influential clusters of similar private eye films emerge. The first is in the classic film noir era, usually declared by critics to extend from around 1940 to 1959. There is then a 'second wave' of films in the late 1960s and '70s which pick up and revise, update and subvert the motifs and themes of this first period. The films produced in these two eras are my main interest in this book because of the features they share and their similar social and aesthetic contexts. In particular, location plays an important role in these movies.

Their settings are more than simply backgrounds, providing atmosphere and suspense; they are subjects of the films themselves. The private eye may be a figure so iconic that his visual image in itself, his very posture and attire, seems sufficient to convey what he stands for, with no background required. Yet if we want to gain a greater understanding of what private eye films tell us, the central character cannot be dissociated from his environment. The private eye movie continually explores the relation between the detective and the world he investigates.

There is a third period in which a large number of private eye movies are produced, but this is much longer and less concentrated: from the 1980s to the present day. We might refer

More than background: the location of *Brick*.

to this period, following theorists of film noir, as the 'neo-noir' era of private detective films. This is a far more disparate and amorphous group of films, characterized either by self-reflexive or parodic treatments of original noir themes or by deliberate attempts to reappropriate the conventions of the private eye film. While this book examines a number of films from this third period, I have resisted the temptation to link them together into a third overall 'moment' because of the considerable aesthetic and socio-historical differences between them. The treatment of location in this third group is much more expansive and diverse.

In any case, these three periods overlap. Robert Altman's *The Long Goodbye* might be said to belong not just to the second wave of private eye films but also to the 'neo-noir' era of parodying the original template, while *Kiss Me Deadly*, though situated historically in the era of film noir, is sufficiently different from other noirs to suggest that it might be an early example of the second wave of private eye movies. Rather than seek to establish rigid boundaries between categories, however, my purpose is to use them merely to introduce a working model of the history of the private eye film which can help the reader to follow the discussion. Nor do I propose to deal exhaustively with each period, still less each of the key films from them. I am more interested in the broader patterns which can be traced in each cinematic moment. While this risks smoothing over the particularities and peculiarities of any individual film, this book is more concerned with what specific private eye movies have in common rather than what distinguishes them.

One common element, which is no doubt already apparent from this introduction, is a connection with noir. I shall say more about this enigmatic category of film in the first chapter. But for now I want to state clearly what my three periods suggest: that the figure of the cinematic private eye is inseparable from film noir.

Joseph Gordon-Levitt as Brendan Fraser in *Brick*.

Private investigation is one of the definitive motifs of film noir in the 1940s and '50s, and the private eye's appearances in later cinema always owe something to this intitial context. He always retains something of his original historical moment, even when he appears in a very different time and place and retains few outward features which identify him as the noir detective. We can see this from the figure's appearance in films as diverse as Rian Johnson's revisionist private eye movie, *Brick* (2005), which transposes the narrative and characters of John Huston's classic film *The Maltese Falcon* (1941) to a present-day Californian high school; fully fledged 'retro-noir' films such as *Angel Heart* (1987) or *Devil in a Blue Dress* (1995); or a comic non-noir movie such as *There's Something About Mary* (1998). As different as these films are from the classic noir template, the depiction of their private eyes mean each includes an implicit commentary on the values associated with noir.

The main task of chapter One is to show how the private eye embodies the desolate, uncertain world which produced film noir. The chapter provides a short history of the private eye movie, or, more precisely, the two major 'moments' in which it burst into life – the 1940s and the '70s – before the passing of its central figure into movie mythology in the decades after. This history will be returned to in the book's Conclusion. Chapter Two considers how the private eye is distinguished from the other species of modern fictional detective, the literary 'armchair' sleuth, and what, consequently, characterizes the narrative in which he features. The private eye is defined chiefly by his 'existential engagement' in the world he investigates, and this means his investigation is less about 'cognition' – or solving a puzzle – than his 'armchair' counterpart.

Chapter Three concentrates on the peculiar dialectic between the worlds of 'work' and 'home' which we find again and again in private eye movies – a theme which is illuminated when we look in detail at the particular locations they choose. As a symbolically 'homeless' figure, the private eye invites viewers to consider the values of 'home' in a fragmented post-war culture. Chapter Four examines the effects of the private eye's incessant work, and suggests this compromises his ability to remain free and clear-sighted in comparison to the 'official' gaze of the police. It also considers the consequences of his work for his own private life and

A classic noir interior space: the detective in the diner in *Angel Heart*.

private desire. This chapter explores the ironic situation mentioned above, in which the man who dedicates his life to penetrating the private lives of others must, as a consequence, forfeit any meaningful private life of his own.

Movie history includes a vast number of films featuring private detectives. It would be impossible, especially in a study of this length, to explore them all, and inevitably I have privileged some over others. Each of the chapters concentrates on a group of related films. In writing the book, I deliberately confined its scope to detectives who are either self-employed or who end up – no matter whether they are professional or amateur – acting as a 'lone wolf', conducting a private investigation without being answerable to anyone else. One of the defining features of the cinematic private eye – along with his mobility, his 'blue collar' status, and his focus on the private realm – is the fact that his detective-work is solitary and personally motivated rather than collective or collaborative.

This decision has tended to keep out the many films which feature police detectives, who work with others as part of a larger operation. It does, however, mean that I can include films such as Otto Preminger's *Laura* (1944), in which the detective Mark McPherson is not technically employed as a private investigator but, because of his personal investment in the case, begins to act like one, and films such as *Rear Window* (1954), *Blue Velvet* (1986) and *Brick*, in which men who are *not* professional private eyes undertake an 'investigation' into a mystery that preoccupies them.

In *Rear Window*, the ironically named police detective Doyle (evocative of the creator of the most famous 'private detective' of them all, Sherlock Holmes) warns the surrogate private eye, Jeffries, against looking too hard into the lives of his neighbours across the yard: 'That's a secret and private world you're looking into out there. People do a lot of things in private that they couldn't explain in public.' His words could serve as the motto for the private eye's detective-work, and it is significant that Jeffries, voyeuristic and entirely private, succeeds in cracking the case where Doyle's official, detached approach to the investigation fails.

Playing detective: the private eye on the bus: Albert Finney as
Eddie Ginley in *Gumshoe*.

I

History: *The Private Eye Film*

'So you're a private detective,' she said. 'I didn't know they
really existed, except in books.'
– Raymond Chandler, *The Big Sleep* (1939)[1]

Literary Origins and the 'Armchair' Detective

Detectives in literature and film fall into one of two main types:
the armchair detective and the private eye. The former is essentially
a nineteenth-century phenomenon, dating back to the pioneering
crime fiction published by the American writer Edgar Allan Poe
in the early 1840s, which gathered together a series of motifs and
characteristics from earlier Gothic and urban tales to create a new
kind of story glorifying the systematic processes of detection.

Poe's stories, 'The Murders in the Rue Morgue' (1841), 'The
Mystery of Marie Rôget' (1842) and 'The Purloined Letter' (1845),
originate the 'logic-and-deduction' (or 'clue-puzzle' or 'whodunnit')
tradition of detective fiction. They introduce the enigmatic
detective, Chevalier Auguste Dupin, an eccentric man of aristocratic
descent who solves crimes – at night, usually in the comfort of his
own room while reading the newspapers for clues, essentially for
the pleasure of exercising his intellect and exposing the weaknesses
of the Paris police. However, it was not until forty years later,
with the advent of Conan Doyle's Sherlock Holmes – 'the most

perfect reasoning and observing machine that the world has seen', as his sidekick Watson puts it[2] – that the conventions of 'logic-and-deduction' detective fiction stabilized into a genre. The genre was formalized further by the Agatha Christie-led golden age of whodunnit detective fiction in the 1920s and '30s.

The origins of private eye fiction are not quite so easy to pinpoint, given that Dupin, Holmes, and Christie's Poirot and Miss Marple are all 'private investigators', working independently of the police. But the private eye tradition begins properly in the 1920s in the U.S., with the appearance of a new breed of 'tough guy' detective, who featured in pulp magazines such as *Black Mask*, *Dime Detective, Detective Fiction Weekly* and *Black Aces*, publications which specialized in a new kind of 'hard-boiled' crime story. The figure then appeared in novels from the late 1920s until the '50s by writers such as Dashiell Hammett, Raymond Chandler and Ross MacDonald. This kind of fiction clearly descended from the Anglo-American classical tradition of Poe and Doyle, given its emphasis on mystery-solving by a single, heroic figure. Yet it also styled itself aggressively as an alternative to what it perceived as the insipid championing of the norms of polite society found in nineteenth-century fiction and, especially, the formulaic mysteries of the classic detective story's heyday.

The hard-boiled detective novel dramatized crime in the style of a thriller rather than as an elaborate parlour game, drawing on the conventions of the romance and adventure story. It also sought to inject a greater degree of realism into its pages by detailing the modern urban world in all its grimy disorder, and featuring a range of characters – low-lifes, dangerously alluring women, corrupt authority figures – who spoke in the street-smart vernacular of contemporary America. This realism and its emphasis on explosive action meant that, without doubt, hard-boiled detective fiction was the crucial influence on private eye cinema. The private eye films dealt with in this book are all descended in some way from the hard-boiled detective story.

Before we begin surveying them, however, it is important to note that, just as the 'logic-and-deduction' form of the detective novel has endured, indeed continued to flourish alongside the hard-boiled variety right up to the present day, so the equivalent cinematic mode has continued to be used in crime films, though much less often. There have been detectives in cinema who are not private eyes, even though they are, technically speaking, 'private detectives'.

Any full survey of detective films would have to begin with Sherlock Holmes. Not surprisingly, because the advent of cinema in the 1890s coincided with the highpoint of Doyle's character's popularity,[3] and because early cinema looked to literature for inspiration, Holmes is the first cinematic detective. He initially appeared on screen in 1903, in *Sherlock Holmes Baffled*, made by the American Biograph Company, and featured in numerous other silent movies made in Denmark, France and Germany (for example, *The Adventures of Sherlock Holmes*, 1905, *Sherlock Holmes and the Great Murder Mystery*, 1908, *Sherlock Holmes in Deathly Danger* and *The Secret Document*, both 1908). The first talking Holmes film was *The Return of Sherlock Holmes* (1929) and this was followed by Doyle-inspired adventures such as *The Scarlet Claw* (1933) and *The House of Fear* (1945). The most famous Holmes film is Twentieth Century Fox's *The Hound of the Baskervilles* (1939), starring Basil Rathbone and Nigel Bruce, a film which actually comes close to *noir* in some of its lighting effects and atmosphere.

The Christie-style model of 'logic-and-deduction' detective fiction has also been well served by the cinema, especially in the 1960s and '70s which saw successful adaptations of Christie novels such as *The Alphabet Murders* (1965), *Murder on the Orient Express*

Debonaire detective: the private eye before film noir. William Powell as Nick Charles in *After the Thin Man* (1936).

(1974) and *Death on the Nile* (1978). Even though, oddly, direct adapations of Christie's work seldom featured in the great advent of Hollywood cinema in the 1930s and '40s (with the exception of *And Then There Were None*, 1945) this period did specialize in gimmicky, light-hearted whodunnits, such as *The Secret of the Blue Room* (1933), *Murder by an Aristocrat* (1936), and *Dr Broadway* (1942). The most successful pre-noir private detective franchises feature the debonair detectives Philo Vance and Nick Charles. Vance, who featured in the novels by 'S. S. Van Dine' (nom de plume of Willard Huntington Wright), and in films such as *The Greene Murder Case* (1929) and *The Gracie Allen Murder Case* (1939), was a self-assured, well-spoken, elegantly dressed descendent of Sherlock Holmes, someone who reasons aloud and mocks the police, who plod in his wake.

Alongside 'armchair' sleuths, early cinema also features a more direct ancestor of the hard-boiled detective. This kind of private investigator, still cultured, ironic, and rather two-dimensional, but with more of a fondness for violence, appeared in cinema with increasing regularity during the rise of the B-movie in the 1930s,[4] especially in various series of 'light-entertainment' mysteries featuring amateur sleuths like Nick Carter (*Nick Carter, Master Detective*, 1939) or Nero Wolfe (*Meet Nero Wolfe*, 1936), investigative figures such as the lawyer Perry Mason, or quasi-mythical crime-solvers such as The Lone Wolf (*The Lone Wolf*, 1924) or The Saint (*The Saint Takes Over*, 1940). Other 'franchises' include the Thatcher Colt series in the early 1930s, the East Asian detectives Charlie Chan and Mr Moto, British detectives like The Falcon, and tough-guy American detectives such as Bulldog Drummond and Boston Blackie.

The Noir Detective

The enduring cinematic version of the private eye emerged with the advent of film noir in the early 1940s. Here is not the place to analyse the historical and aesthetic origins of noir at any length, nor to consider whether or not it is a film genre, a mode, or a more general 'sensibility'. These questions have been explored in exhaustive depth by a large number of critics over the past few decades,[5] and there is a sense that to grapple with them further is to risk becoming lost in a kind of labyrinth of claim and counter-claim which parallels the plight of the typical noir protagonist.

The consensus is that film noir emerged in the U.S. in the 1940s as a reflection of social malaise and economic uncertainty resulting from the Second World War and the impact on cinema of experimental, emotive, aesthetic movements such as German Expressionism. Crucially, the new 1940s 'crime psychology' films (as they were intially termed) were championed by French critics.[6] It is often noted that 'the Americans made [noir] and then the

French invented it'.[7] These critics, caught up in the dark mood of their own nation's social and political climate after the war, felt an affinity with the bleak, violent films being produced in the U.S., and began to analyse their stylistic features and themes, recognizing the link not simply with crime novels by American writers such as Hammett, which provided the source texts of many of the films, but the atmosphere of the hard-boiled literary tradition as a whole. Another contemporary writer, Marcel Duhamel, the promoter of the *série noire* (a series of hard-boiled thrillers, often American fiction in translation, which inspired the label 'film noir'), argued that in these stories we find 'violence – in all its forms, and especially the most shameful – beatings, killings . . . Immorality is as much at home here as noble feelings . . . There is also love – preferably vile – violent passion, implacable hatred.'[8]

Noir is of course French for 'black' and the 'blackness' of noir refers to a number of things. It points to the tradition's roots in Gothic fiction (also called *noir* in French) and its associations

Dectective noir: danger lurks in the private eye's office in *The Dark Corner*.

with the style of popular narrative that James Naremore calls 'blood melodrama'.[9] It denotes the tradition's overall mood of brooding, existential uncertainty, its moral ambivalence, and refusal to provide any form of 'redemption', any 'glimmer of resistance to the dark side' or 're-vindication of society'.[10] It also captures the tenor of the distinctive stylistic features which struck early film critics, such as noir's use of shadows and chiaroscuro lighting, and distorting visual effects.

A fact that cannot be ignored in any analysis of film noir is its stark and provocative sexual politics. Critics recognize that one of the principal motivating factors behind the body of films which make up the category is the need to express a deep anxiety about gender which could not easily be expressed in other ways, especially a crisis in masculine identity. The crisis is usually explained by the shift in gender roles occasioned by America's entry into the Second World War, when women were required to enter the factories to replace the men despatched to the home front, and were then returned to their domestic sphere after the war. This produced in the cultural imaginary a need for cautionary tales about assertive, independent women – a negative fantasy most memorably embodied in another of noir's most enduring character types, the femme fatale. As well as being the product of unique historical factors, this attitude to women conforms to a long-established tendency in Western art and culture to define women in relation to men, and to base this definition on their sexual identity.[11] Essays by feminist critics on noir remind us that the vast majority of women in film noir conform to only two types: 'the exciting, childless whores, or the boring, potentially childbearing sweethearts'.[12]

It is no surprise that the private eye movie, based on the figure of the 'tough guy' detective, exemplifies noir sexual politics especially strongly. Some critics have regarded the 'investigative thriller' as an attempt to reassert masculine identity in the face of the post-war crisis in gender identity. Frank Krutnik argues that central to this kind of film is the 'testing' of a detective 'hero' – 'not merely a testing of his ability as detective . . . but of how he measures up to more extensive standards of masculine competence'.[13]

Where Sherlock Holmes or Hercule Poirot are trustworthy 'gentleman' detectives, the hard-boiled detective – such as Hammett's The Continental Op and Sam Spade, or Raymond Chandler's Philip Marlowe – is notable for his physicality, robust language and action, as well as his moral ambivalence. He is distinguished by what the film writer and director Paul Schrader – fascinated in his own films (for example, *Taxi Driver*, 1976) by vulnerable, violent, men – would describe as 'the "tough", cynical way of acting and thinking which separated one from the world of everyday emotions – romanticism with a protective shell . . . [living] out a narcissistic, defeatist code'.[14] The hard-boiled private eye is not above having sexual liaisons with his clients or suspects and, rather than simply having a different interpretation of a case to that of the police, is frequently in danger of being imprisoned, for they suspect him of deliberately obstructing their investigations. His idealized, uncompromising toughness makes him just as far from a man in the real world as the cerebral armchair detective. Nevertheless, the immersion of the private eye in the dangerous, crime-ridden world which surrounds him makes the novels and films he appears in more of an accurate reflection of twentieth-century urban life than those in the logic-and-deduction tradition. There remains something distinctively and appealingly human about his efforts to get to the bottom of corruption in the face of personal danger. As another of the earliest commentators on noir put it, unlike Sherlock Holmes, this is a detective who 'is not a mechanism but a protagonist'.[15]

Two Kinds of Noir Detective

The tough private detective is undoubtedly one of the classic topoi of film noir, along with the femme fatale, the cornered, doomed hero, and the preoccupation with a claustrophobic, urban world. Surprisingly, however, this status results from only a relatively small number of examples in the classic film noir canon – the films I shall be discussing in this book. The private eye may be ubiquitous in studies of film noir but he is comparatively rare on screen. From the hundreds of films which make up the classic noir canon (according to the various filmographies carefully constructed by critics)[16] only a handful actually feature the private eye as protagonist. Rather than being an irremovable fixture in every world created by film noirs, the private eye is more of a representative figure, someone who encapsulates the qualities of the noir world. His attitude and function in the narrative crystallize wider patterns and themes which can be found in a range of other films. As critics have acknowledged, one of the distinguishing structural features of noir is 'the investigative structure of the narrative' or the 'private investigation quest',[17] and the private eye, as a man who devotes his existence to this quest, therefore embodies one of the central elements of film noir as a whole.

Detectives do frequently crop up as minor characters in film noir, however, as one would expect for a category of film obsessed with crime. We find them, for example, in the films *Scarlet Street* (1945), *Fallen Angel* (1945), *Kiss of Death* (1947) and *Possessed* (1947). And, while independent professional private eyes are relatively scarce, 'investigative protagonists' are everywhere. Characters who play this role include: policemen in *The Black Angel* (1946), *Cry of the City* (1948), *D.O.A.* (1950), *Panic on the Streets* (1950) and *Edge of Doom* (1950); FBI agents in *The Street with No Name* (1948), *The Narrow Margin* (1952), *On Dangerous Ground* (1951) and

A down-at-heel
detective:
Scarlet Street.

Nightmare (1955); insurance agents in *Double Indemnity* (1944)
and *The Killers* (1946); and veteran soldiers in *Cornered* (1945) and
Dead Reckoning (1947). There are many more 'ordinary', doomed
men who find themselves having to prove their innocence or to
find ways of escaping the law after committing a crime.

When it comes specifically to professional private eye
protagonists in classic film noir there are two distinct kinds. The
most iconic type is the intrepid, tough-guy detective drawn from
the fiction of Dashiell Hammett or Raymond Chandler. This is
both the original noir private eye, setting in place conventions
other films will follow – the wisecracking, the womanizing, the
ability to access all the spaces of the city, both affluent and poor
– and the character in its *purest* form, that is, a man who remains
completely professional and independent. He is not in the pay of
any other organization, and also (rather curiously, as I shall argue
in the following chapters) has no private life nor even anything that
suggests much of an *interior* life. For all the noir credentials of
the films he appears in, the narrative in which he is placed resembles
classic 'prose romance', a mode of storytelling which stretches
back to the medieval period and which focuses on the quest

undertaken by an honourable but flawed individual, which includes tests of his moral fortitude.

Hammett's Sam Spade was the first of this new type of detective to feature in film noir,[18] being at the centre of a movie hailed by many as the first proper noir[19] – John Huston's *The Maltese Falcon*, where he was played by Humphrey Bogart. The real fascination in the film is not its two interlinked mysteries (one about the missing 'Maltese Falcon', a priceless artefact, the other about the identity of the person who has killed two men, Thursby and Archer) but Spade himself. He dominates the action and is present in almost every scene, moving from location to location, interviewing, arguing, fighting, cajoling his way through the case. While capable of kindness, he also clearly has a hard, self-centred streak, indicated by the simultaneous affairs he is conducting with three women, and his decision to let one of them, whom he supposedly loves – the femme fatale, Brigid O'Shaughnessy – go to the gallows at the end. The original novel describes him as a 'blond Satan'.[20]

Humphrey Bogart as Sam Spade in *The Maltese Falcon*.

A feature of the film is how adept O'Shaughnessy is at telling stories and play-acting in order to manipulate others or to wriggle out of tricky situations. Yet Spade more than matches her in both respects. Tongue-in-cheek, he tells Dundy and Polhaus, the exasperated police officers who are also on the case, 'Everything can be explained!' His quick-wittedness and steeliness means that even though it is only at the very end that he understands what has been going on, and the band of criminals escape, Spade triumphs. We realize then that what has been at stake all along is not truth or justice, but survival in a battle of desperate individuals.

Despite Spade's moral ambivalence, this film, and the sequence of films featuring Raymond Chandler's detective Philip Marlowe which followed on from its success, create a portrait of the noir detective which is as unproblematically heroic as it could be. The first Marlowe film was *Murder, My Sweet*, Edward Dmytryk's adaptation of Chandler's 1940 novel *Farewell, My Lovely*.[21] This was followed by Howard Hawks's popular version of *The Big*

The detective in the mirror: *The Lady in the Lake*.

Sleep, and two much less successful adaptations: Robert Montgomery's *The Lady in the Lake* (1947), and John Brahm's *The Brasher Doubloon* (1947) (a version of Chandler's *The High Window*, 1942). Although played by a succession of different actors – Bogart again in *The Big Sleep*, Dick Powell in *Murder, My Sweet*, Montgomery himself in *The Lady in the Lake* and George Montgomery (no relation) in *The Brasher Doubloon* – the screen Marlowe in this series of 1940s movies helped cement the Hammett/Chandleresque private eye as an instantly recognizable noir type.

Marlowe is more physically vulnerable than Spade and less sure about the complex intrigues in which he becomes immersed. The plot of *The Maltese Falcon* is self-consciously bewildering (the characters try to figure out a story about a Maltese falcon, while the viewer tries to make sense of a story called *The Maltese Falcon*) but Spade seems to accept the complexity from the outset and is

The private eye interrogated: *Farewell, My Lovely.*

The screen chemistry of Bogart and Bacall: *The Big Sleep*.

able to negotiate its twists and turns through his quick thinking. By contrast, Marlowe frequently seems lost and at the mercy of dark forces which are much more powerful than him. Generically speaking, where Huston's film is essentially a comedy played as a thriller, the Marlowe adaptations are pure 'action-adventure' – albeit a kind inflected with the noir aesthetic and its values. Its protagonist lurches from one dramatic scene to another, encountering hysterical, dissembling women, brutal thugs and the haughty, disingenuous rich, and remains one step behind until the end.

These five films, only three of them commercially successful and critically acclaimed, are the slim body of work on which the cinematic icon of the private eye rests. It is difficult to avoid the conclusion that they became so influential because there was a *need* for such a protagonist in the cultural imaginary – rather than anything especially innovative about them as a genre. What was groundbreaking was their exposition of noir techniques and values. Nevertheless, the 'x factor' behind their influence is undoubtedly the capacity of Bogart, who played both Spade and Marlowe in two of the most celebrated early films, to fulfill the apparent cultural desire for this kind of protagonist. In particular, he had the ability to combine apparent opposites in an enduringly appealing screen persona: tough but fair, cynical but idealistic, shabby and smart, charming and unpleasant (when he needed to be).

The Spade/Marlowe prototype is the most familiar kind of cinematic private eye. But there is also a second type of private detective in classic noir who, in a more understated way, is just as responsible for cementing the figure in screen convention. This is the reluctant or disaffected private investigator, a man who has no alternative but to become a private eye. While he is still brave and capable of acting independently, he represents a more ordinary, workaday side to the profession. He is often a police detective who becomes transformed into a private eye because of what

Cast adrift: the private eye on the train (*The Narrow Margin*).

happens to him in the narrative. Because there is something personal about the investigation he is involved in, he is compelled to start working as a solitary investigator, cast adrift from the force which employs him. We find this kind of detective in movies such as *Laura*, *The Dark Corner* (1946), *The Narrow Margin* and *The Big Heat* (1953). In *The Narrow Margin*, for example, Detective Sergeant Brown is effectively pushed into playing the role of private eye by his own police force, that has had him watched by an undercover police officer who is pretending to be the woman he is supposed to protect.

But there is also the independent professional investigator forged from the same prototype as Spade or Marlowe, but who is less glamorous and heroic than either, more corruptible, and more of a failure. The prime example here is Bailey in *Out of the Past*. He is essentially a good man, but unable to prevent himself from mixing with the wrong company. Some police detectives or cops in film noir, it must be said, are unequivocally 'bad men' – such as those in *I Wake Up Screaming* (1941), *Where the Sidewalk Ends* (1950), *On Dangerous Ground*, *Shield for Murder* (1954) and *Touch of Evil* (1958). None of these, however, are protagonists in the kind of investigative plot that typifies the private eye movie.

These two kinds of detective – self-employed 'lone wolf', and disaffected policeman – are the figures who emerge from the first 'wave' of private eye films, part of classic noir in the 1940s and '50s. For all their credentials as men of action, both types remind us that private detection is a mundane, at times unpleasant, job rather than a vocation bestowed upon a man by a sense of higher moral purpose. Private investigation is a kind of hard, unrewarding labour, and the significance of work in the private eye movie is something I shall return to in chapter Three.

While they exude a toughness and vitality, noir detectives are further from the confident, invulnerable masculine ideal advanced

The sadistic private eye: Hammer in *Kiss Me Deadly*.

by hard-boiled 'pulp' literature than one might think. Bogart's portrayals in *The Maltese Falcon* and *The Big Sleep* amount to the only real embodiment of this masculine ideal, with other similar detectives actually to be found closer to the two opposite ends of the pole between sensitivity and brutality. Marlowe in *Murder, My Sweet* is edgy and restless, and in *The Lady in the Lake* has turned to writing novels and thinking of settling down for good with Adrienne Fromsett. Both these films contain prolonged masochistic sequences which demonstrate the detective's susceptibility to emasculation. At the other extreme, the private eye Mike Hammer, who appears in *I, The Jury* (1953) and, most memorably, in Robert Aldrich's apocalyptic Cold War detective noir *Kiss Me Deadly* (1955), pushes the ideal of masculine power so far that it becomes almost psychopathic.

Hammer was the creation of the right-wing hard-boiled writer Mickey Spillane, who transformed the fearless, wandering Chandleresque detective into a violent, xenophobic misogynist, in a series of best-selling novels in the early 1950s. Hammer's sadistic attitude to others is exemplified in the scene in *Kiss Me Deadly* in which he shuts a coroner's hand in a drawer to force him to give up the key to a safety deposit box, grinning cruelly while the woman he is with, Lily Carver, covers her ears to block out the man's screams. Throughout the movie, his voracious sexual appetite is conveyed in metaphors about eating: he tells his secretary/girlfriend Velda that 'just the soft part of your arm is like a meal'; when kissing another woman, he talks of how she 'tastes wonderful', then comes back for 'seconds'; and when watching a group of girls pass by, he remarks 'ooh, look at those goodies!'

Hammer's hypermasculinity is the exception that proves the rule, however. Other noir detectives are far less violent, insensitive and uncompromising, and indeed less 'untarnished and unafraid' than one would expect from Chandler's polemical portrait of the private eye in 'The Simple Art of Murder' (1944).[22]

The Return of the Noir Detective

James Naremore has argued that the portrayal of Hammer in *Kiss Me Deadly*, as well as the movie's continual references to Greek mythology, classical music and art, signal that the film is a carefully constructed 'critique of Spillane', an unashamedly 'uncultured' writer.[23] There is certainly an air of parody about the private eye in *Kiss Me Deadly*, which indicates that cinema was already beginning to revise and challenge the model of the private detective in the classic noir period. It was not until the 1970s, however, that this became a task taken up by film-makers in significant enough numbers that it comes to seem something like a 'project'. Following a decade-long hiatus in which few private eye movies of note were released, the noir private eye was resurrected in a series of films in the late 1960s and '70s: *Marlowe* (1969), *Chandler* (1972), *The Long Goodbye*, *Shamus* (1973), *Chinatown* and *Farewell, My Lovely*.

As the first two titles show, these films self-consciously meditate the importance of Chandler in American culture. Each of the others is an adaptation of a Chandler novel, while the word 'shamus', popular slang for detective, is uttered by Marlowe in *The Big Sleep*. The detectives in these films are Chandleresque, too, in that they are even further from the tough guy, and closer to the wandering hero of the romance (as I shall explain more in the next chapter) than movies of the 1940s. Other, less Chandleresque but equally important, private eye films of the period include *Klute* (1971), *Night Moves* (1975), *The Drowning Pool* (1975) and *The Big Fix* (1978). The film which figures as the 'bridge' between classic noir and the second wave is Jack Smight's *Harper*. Based on *The Moving Target* (1949), a novel by one of the other great writers of hard-boiled detective fiction, Ross MacDonald, the movie tells a complex missing-persons story which recalls *Murder, My Sweet* and *The Big Sleep*. It does so with a lightly ironic tone, and provides a disapproving portrayal of the garish 1960s bohemian world which is very much of its time. Its downbeat ending reveals the ultimate impotence of the private eye, and thus sets the tone for the 1970s private eye movies, showing their interest in refashioning the private eye for a new era rather than simply echoing classic noir.

Paul Newman as Lew Harper in *Harper*.

These films are all 'neo-noirs' in some respects. This label tends to be used by film critics to refer to film noirs produced after the classical period of film noir, those which project the original 'narrative and stylistic conventions . . . onto a contemporary canvas'.[24] As one would expect, the long period from 1960 to the present involves considerable shifts of emphasis in cinema, and a vast number of very different films, so there has naturally been considerable debate about exactly which trends and sub-genres constitute 'neo-noir'. This is another debate we do not need to get too involved in here, given that our focus is purely on the private eye movie. Andrew Spicer usefully divides neo-noir into two main periods: the 'neo-modernist' noir period, which stretches from the mid-1960s until the end of the 1970s (though he includes a number of French and Italian new wave antecedents, which are roughly contemporaneous with classic noir), and the 'postmodern' period, stretching from the 1980s to the early 2000s.

The second wave of private eye movies is clearly 'neo-modernist' in Spicer's terms. Neo-modernism in cinema is more experimental than mainstream film, and is preoccupied with investigating 'the relationship between representation and reality' and by 'the problems of identity and memory'. Neo-modern forms of cinema thus tend to depict 'unmotivated characters adrift in ambiguous situations beyond their comprehension which they are incapable of resolving'.[25] They display what Fredric Jameson termed 'the great modernist thematics of alienation, anomie, solitude, social fragmentation and isolation'.[26]

In America in the late 1960s and '70s, Spicer argues, a group of directors – some young, such as Arthur Penn (*Night Moves*), some established, such as Robert Altman (*The Long Goodbye*), some European émigrés, such as Roman Polanski (*Chinatown*) – were able to exploit the control ceded to them by studios worried by declining audience figures, to produce neo-modernist-influenced films which combined absorbing narratives with typically neo-modernist formal innovations like 'disjunctive editing . . . hand-held camera-work, very long takes . . . and a consistent preference for long shots'.[27]

The second wave of private eye movie marries such devices to thriller conventions.[28] They cast bankable new stars who combine sex appeal with gravitas: Paul Newman, James Garner, Elliott Gould, Jack Nicholson, Gene Hackman. Their narratives are broadly similar to the original noir movies and their hard-boiled source texts. The detective is a solitary, independent figure, usually despatched on a missing-persons case (a staple of hard-boiled plotting that, to a neo-modernist sensibility, carries with it suggestive connotations of an identity-crisis), who fearlessly struggles to piece together information in the face of attempts by brutal criminals to violently throw him off the scent, and by the police to keep him away from their investigation. Often in these films, however, this is because the real crime is perpetrated by the rich and powerful, and the police are either in league with more powerful forces or have become used to turning a blind eye. As in the original film noirs, the private eye's quest involves constantly, restlessly, moving from one location to another, tailing suspects, engaging in surveillance work, interviewing suspects and trying to glean information from shady authority figures.

The chief difference between second wave films and their classic noir predecessors is that the atmosphere of social alienation and degeneration seems to weigh heavily on the shoulders of the private eye, who becomes a sorry figure at times: anachronistic, lonely, ineffectual, in the grip of an existential crisis, treated con-temptuously by those he comes into contact with. He might still be considered 'heroic' in some ways – he remains a man of action, and remains comfortable with violence, as well as being attractive to women – but is in fact more reminiscent of the anti-heroes of modernist fiction and film. His heroism comes from his status as a social outsider who brings into focus the social malaise of his age, bravely managing to *survive* it without succumbing to it and becoming one of 'them'.

The finest example of this downscaled private eye is Elliott Gould's shambling, laconic, slightly bewildered Philip Marlowe in Robert Altman's masterful *The Long Goodbye*. The contrast with the sharp, weasley, energetic Marlowe played by Bogart could not be more stark. In his values, Chandler's detective was always out of step with his cynical, morally vacuous age, both in the original novels and the 1940s screen adaptations. But this Marlowe is made to *look* deliberately out of place. Against the backdrop of a bohemian Los Angeles suburb in the 1970s he drives a vintage 1948 Lincoln Continental, and dresses in a shabby 1940s suit and tie (printed with stars and stripes) which make him look absurdly formal: at one point, the man he has been tasked to find, Wade, urges him to take the tie off, for this reason. His incompatibility with the modern world signals that this is more than simply someone who stands for values which are now defunct, but an impossible fantasy figure, one who belongs to an earlier celluloid era, and is entirely unsuited to the real world. This is how other characters respond to him, too – either as a harmless curio ('A private eye with a private elevator!') or as a man deserving of contempt ('your friend Marlowe, the do-good bullshitter, or whatever he is').

Other films carried the faint air of ridiculousness in *The Long Goodbye* into outright comedy. *The Late Show* (1977) was a comic-elegiac treatment of the ageing, out-of-place private eye. Stephen Frears's *Gumshoe* (1971) was a parodic noir about an unemployed, aspiring stand-up comic, who becomes a private investigator after placing an ad in the local newspaper. He dresses in a trenchcoat, yet still travels by bus, and uses his dole card as his investigator's

ID. The film really belongs to the tradition of British Northern, picaresque, working-class, kitchen-sink fiction, à la Keith Waterhouse's 1959 novel *Billy Liar*, and the comedy comes from how unsuited the British location is to the world of the gumshoe.[29]

Other major films in the second wave also present the detective as powerless and lost in a world which he cannot understand or alter, though more subtly than *The Long Goodbye* or comedies like *Gumshoe*. Jake Gittes spends most of *Chinatown* mistaken about the nature of the case he is investigating, and when he finally realizes the truth he is unable to change anything or bring anyone to justice. Similarly, Lew Harper in *Harper* discovers that the murderer he had been looking for is none other than one of his closest friends, the lawyer and aspirant politician Albert Graves, and decides he is unable to turn him in. Harry Moseby, the private eye in Arthur Penn's *Night Moves*, is powerless to prevent a series of deaths and to smash the brutal smugglers' ring it turns out he is dealing with, and ends the film lying on a boat wounded – genuinely hurt, but symbolically a lame duck. Even Dick Richards's version of *Farewell, My Lovely* – the third adaptation of Chandler's novel – which features a less incongruous 1940s Marlowe (the film is set in Los Angeles in 1941, curiously and inexplicably just two years after the date of the original novel), is pervaded by a wistful air, not unlike *The Long Goodbye*. The effect of the 57-year-old Robert Mitchum playing Marlowe, who acknowledges in the film that he is 'growing old', is to suggest that that the species of detective he represents is on the point of extinction.

One reason for the anachronistic, near-extinct air of these Chandleresque private eyes is that the crime film in the 1970s had hit on a new kind of action-hero law-broker: the rogue cop, ruthless, corruptible, brutally violent, and happy to use any methods that worked to solve the crime, no matter how unethical. This kind of lone hero featured in *Dirty Harry* (1971) (and its sequels,

Magum Force, 1973, *The Enforcer*, 1976, and *Sudden Impact*, 1983),
The French Connection (1971), *Across 110th Street* (1972), *The Seven-
Ups* (1973), *The Choirboys* (1977) and *The Gauntlet* (1977), and, in
comparison, the private eye seemed an irrelevant museum-piece.

Klute provided a complement to the out-of-sync Chandleresque private eye by placing an underqualified and underexpe-
rienced private detective in a dark psycho-killer movie, while a
notable reappropriation of the genre, which conformed to the conventions of the pacy, violent rogue cop film, is the movie *Shaft*,
released in 1971. This film initiates the blaxploitation genre –
films explicitly made for black audiences in the 1970s, featuring
funk-jazz soundtracks and glorying in the deliberately antagonis-
tic behaviour of their black protagonists. The eponymous private
eye John Shaft embodied all the idealistic heroism of the original
'tough guy' tradition in pulp literature, but in a way which still
implied a critique of the classic noir detective tradition, for blackness is conspicuous by its absence from the cultural milieu of noir
in general and from private detective films in particular.

The interest directors like Gordon Park (*Shaft*) and Robert
Altman (*The Long Goodbye*) had in reappropriating the conventions
of the original private eye movie is typical of film-making in the
1970s. Film noir, more than other genres (such as the Western, for

Donald Sutherland as John Klute in *Klute*.

The epitome of cool: Richard Roundtree as John Shaft in *Shaft*.

example), was a critical construction; a category imposed onto a body of films by later critics rather than a set of conventions 1940s film-makers consciously adhered to. To a generation of directors working from the 1970s to the '90s, film noir was a label in the history of film they were well aware of. It was something many of them had studied at film school or watched avidly in order to learn their craft. It was simply impossible for a Robert Altman or a Roman Polanski to make a private eye movie without being conscious of the tradition into which their film fitted and wanting to *use* the genre for their own ends.

This accounts for the strong degree of self-reflexivity displayed in the second wave private eye canon. Self-reflexive elements range from light intertextual touches within the films, such as Eddie Ginley in *Gumshoe* wishing he had written *The Maltese Falcon*, to ironic comments on the genre, such as Marlowe in *The Long Goodbye* exclaiming, while being interrogated by police, 'Is this where I'm supposed to say "what's all this about?", and he says "shut up, I ask the questions"?' The title of *Night Moves*, though it connotes the kind of nefarious activities generated by crime and sexual infidelity (both central to the plot), refers most obviously to chess, in particular the 'knight moves' (used in the chess game Moseby is playing against himself in one scene) which recall Chandler's *The Big Sleep*. In this novel Marlowe is cast as the anachronistic knight, trying in vain to uphold traditional moral values in a brutal world. In Arthur Penn's later film, not only is the quest impossible – and the chess game unwinnable – but its 'knight'-detective is even less worthy of the title than his predecessor.

Postmodern Private Eyes

This kind of self-reflexive homage to classic private eye movies (and indeed the second wave tradition itself) is a common feature of the detective movies made in the period which followed: from the 1980s to the present day. The practice might be regarded as confirmation that the aesthetic climate in which these movies of the past three decades has been made is that of postmodernism. Postmodern culture is the climate in which those who produce artistic work, whether it is literature, film, visual art or architecture, do so in the knowledge of the traditions which precede them and consequently their work advertises that fact either through subtle or obvious references or through more elaborate intertextual homage to a previous work.

Two examples of this latter practice in private eye cinema are Carl Reiner's 1982 parody *Dead Men Don't Wear Plaid*, which makes fun of typical private eye conventions such as the relationship between detective and femme fatale, and comically splices in to its black-and-white diegesis actual footage from eighteen classic noir

Dead Men Don't Wear Plaid: a parody of detective noir.

films, and Shane Black's *Kiss Kiss Bang Bang* (2005), in which a criminal evades the police by auditioning on impulse for a film role as a noir private eye, only later to be mistaken for one and become involved in a real investigation. Ironically, the films only make sense fully (the jokes work) when read against the previous tradition of private eye movies.

This extensive parodic strategy is often found in postmodern literature,[30] in postmodern cinema generally, and in recent private eye cinema specifically, but much more common are the kinds of self-reflexive gestures which we noted above in second wave

A parodic private eye: Robert Downey Jr as Harry Lockhart in *Kiss Kiss, Bang Bang*.

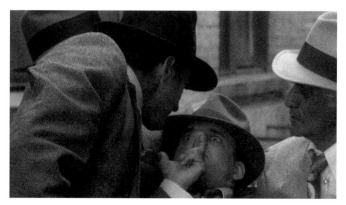

Dead Men Don't Wear Plaid.

movies such as *The Long Goodbye* – those which contribute to the meanings viewers can derive from the narrative, but which do not entirely deconstruct the movie by making it ultimately only 'about' cinema. Even if a viewer happened to be unaware of the noir tradition of private eye films *The Long Goodbye* evokes (though it is hard to imagine what kind of viewer this might be, apart from a very young one), it would still be a powerful piece of cinema in its own right. Without knowledge of the source texts, *Dead Men Don't Wear Plaid* would lose much of its comedy.

Another example of the more judicious use of intertextual allusion would be the succession of references to the most iconic image in *Chinatown* (itself a partly knowing commentary on the noir movie) – the moment when the director Polanski, in a cameo role as a vindictive hoodlum, slices open one side of Jake Gittes's nose: 'You know what happens to nosy fellas? . . . They lose their noses!' The episode is echoed in *Angel Heart* when Harry Angel briefly wears a nose-block a vendor has given him on the beach, in *Manorama Six Feet Under* (2007), when the original scene is playing on the protagonist's TV, and in *Brick*, when the surrogate private eye Brendan's nose is broken.

'You know what happens to nosy fellas?' (Polanski's cameo in *Chinatown*).

Angel Heart, evoking *Chinatown*.

An Indian take on *Chinatown*: *Manorama: Six Feet Under*.

We might recognize in such playful elements the distinctly postmodern kind of nostalgia for a prior cultural tradition forever out of reach for the current generation, who are fated to come after those really capable of pioneering and innovating. More relevant to my discussion in this book, however, are films in the most recent period which set about revising aspects of the private eye genre either by reworking them, combining them with the conventions of another genre, or by picking out a convention and taking it in a new direction.

Examples of the first kind of revisionary practice are movies which recast the private eye as either black or female. As a complement to *Shaft*, Carl Franklin's *Devil in a Blue Dress* invites viewers to reflect upon the absence of black detectives in original noir by depicting an African-American version of the Chandleresque private eye in LA in the 1940s. The late 1980s and early '90s saw a number of films which revised the investigative detective movie from a feminist viewpoint, featuring women in the key roles. Interestingly, apart from *V. I. Warshawski* (1991), an adaptation of Sara Paretsky's 1984 novel *Deadlock*, these investigative women

The black private eye: Denzel Washington as Easy Rawlins in *Devil in a Blue Dress*.

are not usually self-employed independent detectives but tend to work undercover, as if to emphasize the role of the feminine in the detective movie, which is often to subtly undercut masculine pretensions. Thus there is a female narcotics agent in *Fatal Beauty* (1987), a female agent of the Justice Department in *Black Widow* (1987), a female FBI undercover agent in *Betrayed* (1988) and a female undercover police officer in *Impulse* (1990). In addition, female cops feature in *The Silence of the Lambs* (1990), *Blue Steel* (1989) and *Fargo* (1996).[31] Most of these films, however, conform more to the conventions of other sub-genres of the crime film, such as the police procedural, the cop movie or the serial killer film, rather than portraying a female equivalent of the Chandleresque private eye hero. The dearth of 'true' female cinematic private eyes emphasizes how unalterably androcentric the tradition is.

Some of the most notable private eye films of the past few decades are those which blend the private eye film with another genre, a practice which has been related to postmodernism and termed 'hybridization',[32] because the melding of two cinematic genres means that viewers automatically read the film as an implicit commentary on cinema itself as much as an exploration of other issues. The most celebrated example of the hybridized private eye movie is Ridley Scott's cyberpunk movie *Blade Runner* (1982), which sets the private eye narrative in a future LA, in 2019. The location itself is enough to point to a parallel with the private eye tradition, as LA was Marlowe's city. Its detective, Rick Deckard, is partly a rewired Philip Marlowe and partly (as his name suggests) an ironic reincarnation of the great philosopher René Descartes, tasked with testing the difference between reality and fake as he investigates whether 'replicants', robots used for dangerous or menial tasks on the other planets which have been colonized by Earth, are trying to return and pass themselves off as humans.[33]

Sci-fi private eye: Harrison Ford as Deckard in *Blade Runner*.

Other hybrid private eye movies include *Angel Heart*, which combines the hard-boiled detective story with the horror film, showing a detective investigating a series of horrific murders in Voodoo country in Louisiana, and the more recent *Brick*, which juxtaposes private eye conventions with those of the high-school movie and thereby invites a fresh reading of the hard-boiled

Eddie Constantine as private detective Lemmy Caution in Godard's hard-boiled sci-fi hybrid *Alphaville* (1965).

detective movie by showing a teenager taking on the role of investigator. The figure of the private eye becomes defamiliarized as an adolescent traversing the adult world, morally pure, though frequently tempted by impurities, and without any reliable authority figure to turn to for help.

Brick is also an example of a distinctive mini-tradition within the private eye movie in which an ordinary person takes on the role of private investigator and deploys the techniques of the private detective. Ostensibly, this is to solve a mystery he has stumbled upon. As the film develops, however, the viewer suspects it is really about indulging in their own private fantasy. In one sense the amateur detective narrative is a development of one of the staple plots in film noir, in which a man is forced to undertake an investigation to save his life or to prevent himself being framed. In *D.O.A.*, for example, Frank Bigelow finds out that he has been poisoned and has only a matter of days to live, so he desperately has to find who is responsible and why.

This amateur-detective plot was made into an art by Alfred Hitchcock. Rather than official detectives, who are surprisingly thin on the ground in the work of a director so associated with crime films,[34] the 'detective-work' in Hitchcock is usually engaged in by the ordinary man, who is drawn into a complex web of intrigue which he cannot understand, having to evade the grasp of criminals and often the law in order to expose the guilty one so he can exonerate himself. Two Hitchcock films in particular, *Rear Window* and *Vertigo* (1958), feature ordinary men 'playing detective', but in a game where the stakes are fatally high.

One of the finest post-Hitchcock examples of this strain of films is David Lynch's disturbing neo-noir *Blue Velvet* in which an adolescent (like the hero of *Brick*), Jeffrey Beaumont, finds a severed ear in a park and tries to determine whose it is, using stock-in-trade techniques which he has no doubt learned from

'Film blanc': Brendan causes an accident in *Brick*.

the movies (in one scene the noir thriller *This Gun for Hire* is on the TV in his house) such as tailing suspects, inveigling his way into private apartments and taking photographs from a camera concealed in a shoebox. Beaumont demonstrates that the techniques of the private eye do not have to be deployed by a professional to 'work' – though his amateur status casts doubt on his motives. How far the detective's desire might divert the course of his investigation is an interesting question, which will be returned to in chapter Four.

The cinematic private eye is a figure who becomes inscribed into the cultural consciousness by a handful of key film noirs in the 1940s and '50s, and then is depicted as an irrelevance or a curio by a series of often brilliant neo-modernist noirs in the 1970s. From the 1980s on (and the story will be brought up to date in the concluding chapter of this book) the self-reflexive dimension of movies like *Blue Velvet* and *Brick* shows how firmly set in film lore the private eye remains, despite the fact that he was redundant almost before he became essential. Throughout his cinematic life, just as important as his iconicity and the appeal of his romantic individualism has always been the question of how the private eye relates to the world in which he is placed, and how this enables viewers to reflect on aspects of their own world, especially its private sphere. This is what the rest of this book will consider, beginning, in the next chapter, by exploring the private eye's techniques and their complex relation to mystery solving.

Spying: *The Big Sleep*.

2

Seeing: *Literature, Film and the World of the Private Eye*

'You may think you know what you're dealing with, but, believe me, you don't.' – *Chinatown*

Alternative Origins: The X-ray Detective

Hard-boiled detective fiction emerged as a challenge to classic Anglo-American fiction, a corrective to the tradition initiated by Edgar Allan Poe and developed by Arthur Conan Doyle and later writers such as Agatha Christie, Dorothy L. Sayers and John Dickson Carr. But, like its 'soft-boiled' counterpart, the genre descends from Poe – not from his Dupin stories, but from a tale he published in 1840, 'The Man of the Crowd'. This is the story of a prototypical detective, whose suspicions are aroused by an old man he watches and then pursues relentlessly through London streets for almost 24 hours in order to find out his secret. The protagonist becomes more and more agitated as his quarry traverses the streets, changing direction on a whim, before he eventually decides that the old man, the 'man of the crowd', is like an 'unreadable' text.[1]

The story was famously described by the cultural theorist Walter Benjamin as an 'X-ray picture of a detective story',[2] as if it were the basic skeleton from which detective fiction 'proper' emerged. Benjamin suggests that the story captures, like a historical snapshot, the precise moment at which one mythical urban figure mutates into another. The *flâneur*, a man who strolled comfortably through the city streets, reading the chaotic urban environment and its diverse inhabitants as if they constituted a legible 'text', became the fearless solver of crimes, the detective.

Commonly read as a detective story lacking a detective, 'The Man of the Crowd' might instead be considered a fledgling private eye story. Noting the fact that the pursuant is shod in 'caoutchouc overshoes',[3] Patricia Merivale has suggested that Poe's story provides us with the first 'gumshoe' story in fiction.[4] Examined closely, it rehearses just as many of the key properties of later hard-boiled crime fiction – and noir private eye movies – as the original Dupin tales prefigure the conventions of armchair detective fiction. An investigator, cast out on the mean streets rather than enjoying the refuge of a safe home or workplace, tails a suspect whom he believes is involved in some obscure criminal activity, but is unable to fathom it out completely. He is also an example of an ordinary man compelled to 'play detective'. This narrative trajectory is accompanied by other distinctly 'noir' features: the way the story is 'lit' (by 'the rays of the gaslamp' which 'threw over every thing a fitful and garish lustre'), the labyrinthine plot which envelops the investigator, and the suspicion that he himself, obsessed and disoriented, is somehow implicated.[5]

'The Man of the Crowd' has also been plausibly linked to the origins of cinema. Tom Gunning has elaborated on Benjamin's idea that film was the perfect medium for a newly urban society conditioned by 'perception in the form of shocks'.[6] He argues that people were – like the narrator of Poe's story – experiencing the excitement of city life, the teeming crowds, the goods in shops framed by brightly lit windows, and so on, in ways which prefigured the absorption of the viewer of film in the spectacle on screen. 'The Man of the Crowd' might therefore fruitfully be read as a kind of dream of the future medium of cinema: a viewer begins in front of a large window frame watching a lit spectacle and becomes so entranced by it that he is compelled to enter the action himself.[7]

What strengthens the idea that this 1840 story, written 100 years before the advent of film noir, is the first private eye 'film' is the particular kind of detective-work deployed by its hero. His method is not to take account of the details overlooked by others like Dupin or Sherlock Holmes, and sift rationally through the clues. Poe's early private eye deploys a more immediate, intensely focused and less discerning visual technique: keeping the object of his investigation in his gaze in a way which more closely resembles the fascinated gaze of the voyeur than the detached observation of the armchair detective. Another parallel would be with the restlessly mobile and prurient gaze of the movie camera, and this similarity to the cinematic apparatus is one reason why the hard-boiled private eye story came to dominate the detective film rather than the logic-and-deduction variety, where the gaze of the detective is more like that associated with Foucault's panopticon, dispassionate and panoramic. In classic detective fiction the gaze of the detective remains, in any case, largely implicit.

'The Man of the Crowd' points to an interesting doubleness about the private eye's viewing gaze, something that, paradoxically, makes it both especially accurate and not accurate enough. It has the capacity to view closely, to see what other people miss. Yet precisely because of this closeness it can only provide partial vision, never the complete picture. Even though Poe's narrator's technique of close scrutiny is developed and refined in the professional private eye, the bearer of the private eye's gaze is always a single individual, privately employed and with limited access to a community of other viewers, such as police colleagues. The intrigue of a private eye film, I think, owes a great deal to this paradox as we follow in the footsteps of a figure who alternatively reveals things and is unable to grasp their full significance. This chapter examines in more detail what distinguishes the private eye, the 'x-ray detective', from his 'armchair' counterpart, and considers the kind of narrative he features in and how viewers are invited to respond to it.

From the Armchair to the Mean Streets

For a good 80 years the private eye has been a stock cinematic type, one continually revised, critiqued and parodied in different cinematic eras and modes. From its early days in the mid-1940s, film noir criticism has tended to see this type as promoting a powerful image of masculine identity, one which both aggressively asserts the value of the 'tough guy' approach to the world and, in doing so, reveals how it is under threat from this world. It is often assumed that the crime narrative which drives the private eye film is just a smokescreen for what *really* matters deeper within: its playing-out of a fantasy narrative about masculinity. Thus Christine Gledhill argues that 'the processes of detection – following clues and deductive intelligence – are submerged by the hero's relations with the woman he meets and it is the vagaries of this relationship that determine the twists and turns of the plot'.[8] Frank Krutnik contends that 'what is at stake in the private-eye story is not the safeguarding of "normal" society' but 'the affirmation of the hero as an idealised and undivided figure of masculine potency and invulnerability'.[9]

There is no doubt that such insight into questions of gender and sexuality in private eye movies has helped us understand how film noir mediates masculine and feminine ideals. Yet to assume that the detective-work undertaken by the private eye is really about anxiety – and wider cultural anxieties – about gender, overlooks other implications of the 'private eye function' in film.

Bogart as Sam Spade in *The Maltese Falcon*.

I will come to these other implications later in the book. As a prelude, though, I want here to examine a notable feature of the private eye film: how the private detective relates to the world in which he finds himself. Unlike the armchair detective, he is fully *engaged* in this world. Yet, because of this engagement, he effectively cannot see what is right in front of his eyes. He is at once a seeing and a non-seeing detective.

In his novel *City of Glass* (1985), an unusual literary appropriation of the conventions of detective fiction rather than a straightforward piece of 'genre-fiction', Paul Auster describes the symbolic appeal of the detective for his protagonist, a novelist who impulsively takes on a missing-person case following a misdirected phone call:

Private eye. The term held a triple meaning for Quinn. Not only was it the letter 'i', standing for 'investigator', it was 'I' in the upper case, the tiny life-bud buried in the body of the breathing self. At the same time, it was also the physical eye of the writer, the eye of the man who looks out from himself into the world and demands that the world reveal itself to him. For five years now, Quinn had been living in the grip of this pun.[10]

The idea of looking out into the world demanding it reveal its secrets sums up the function of the private eye in hard-boiled fiction and film. It recalls what happens in 'The Man of the Crowd' – and also hints at the existential consequences of this activity, the fact that investigation involves uncovering truths about the detective's own identity. But what is clear from Auster's novel, which documents a complete failure to understand what the case involves, never mind solve it, is that what matters to the private eye is the process of exposing the world's secrets – not the secrets themselves.

It is not quite accurate to call the private eye – as the literary theorist Brian McHale has done – a 'cognitive-hero',[11] a man who is a 'cognizer of the world and agent of *re*cognitions (Aristotelian *anagnorisis*)'.[12] The private eye movie is much less interested in cognition, the process of rational understanding, even the solution to a mystery, than it might seem. More pertinent is the private eye's capacity to expose aspects of the world he enters, to *unveil* what goes on in its locations. Undoubtedly, one consequence of this (as I shall explore in the next chapter) is the intrusive unveiling of *feminine* space. Yet this is really a problematic part of a more universal function performed by the private eye: to reveal to the viewer's gaze a dysfunctional, barred or inaccessible domestic world.

I noted in the previous chapter that there are two kinds of detective, the armchair detective and the hard-boiled private eye.

Despite the obvious differences in class (upper class versus 'blue collar'), nationality (European versus American), nature (cerebral versus physical), and morality (upstanding versus ambivalent), in one respect they are variations on the same archetype. Neither is publicly employed: Dupin, Holmes and Poirot also work 'privately', conducting an alternative investigation to the official one run by the police. Both kinds of detective apply cognitive skills to the mystery which confronts them. Though they do not have a 'method' to adhere to in the way Sherlock Holmes does, Spade, Marlowe, Hammer, Klute, Gittes, and so on, have a keen eye for detail, and frequently, like Holmes, notice what others miss. Both, too, place a world under investigation.

But here we come to the most significant difference between the two varieties of detective fiction. Their worlds – both in terms of the specific places which constitute each world, and the more general 'kind of environment' each is – are radically unlike each other. In Doyle or Christie, as in the Philo Vance or 'Thin Man' movie franchises, the world is a rarefied one of vicarages, drawing rooms, upper-class dining carriages, or well-appointed apartments, plush hotels and dinner parties – a real world perhaps, but one out of kilter with the existence of the majority in the twentieth century, and only accessible to a certain class of person. By contrast, hard-boiled fiction and film noir were acclaimed from the outset for their unflinching portrait of a realistic, modern world. 'It is not a very fragrant world', Chandler writes in 'The Simple Art of Murder', but 'it is the world you live in'.[13]

In fact the noir world is just as heavily stylized and unrealistic as the cosy world of armchair detective fiction. But in giving it the appearance of the world the viewers either knew, or believed was out there in the turbulent 1940s, film noir retained the flavour of realism. The actual locations chosen by noir directors contribute just as powerfully to the feel of the movies as the famed visual techniques (skewed, distorted or reflected images, extreme close-ups and irregular framing, for example) or moody soundtracks (melancholy jazz scores, discordant effects, and so on). These settings, in the 1940s at least, owed something to the impoverished conditions of the time: the low-budget, wartime B-movie made unavoidable such cost-cutting exercises as shooting 'day-for-night' (making daytime seem like night by using a filter) and building stark, spare sets. The result is the striking interiors which characterize film noir: the private spaces, such as narrow corridors, darkened apartments, out-of-the-way wooden shacks, abandoned warehouses, rooms furnished only with simple tables and chairs and lit by a bare bulb, and the down-at-heel public spaces, such as the dimestore, the card school, the boxing ring, the nightclub, the diner or the bar.

Then there are the exteriors, the empty, desolate, rain-soaked streets, the dark alleyways, the shadowy neighbourhoods lit – ostensibly by street lamps – as if they were expectant stage sets. When there are people in these scenes, they tend to be solitary and still: they stand under lamp posts, hang about in doorways,

A typical 'noirscape': the opening of *The Killers*.

or appear through fog. One of the bywords for film noir is 'urban', but actually the outside spaces in noir tend to be 'downtown' or 'suburban': noir narratives are acted out by people who live on the margins.

One of these characters is the detective, and he is no more likely to escape this desolate world than any other of its inhabitants. Noir locations were never quite as sparse from the 1950s on, as a result of increased budgets and advances in film technique. The apartments in 1950s private eye films, such as *The Big Heat* and *Kiss Me Deadly*, are more believably individualized, while both interior and exterior spaces are rendered in colourful detail in second wave movies such as *Harper* or *Chinatown*. Yet these films still convey the sense that the private eye would be unable to extricate himself from the world he investigates even if he tried.

'The Story of the Vulnerable Detective'

Not only are the settings of noir and the classic whodunnit worlds apart, the detectives who preside over each kind of story relate to their world differently. The distinction can be suggested metonymically by two locations: the 'armchair', signifying the safe, homely space, where the detective removes himself from the world he investigates and draws his conclusions, and the 'mean streets', which the private eye must traverse.

In championing the non-fragrant world of the hard-boiled novel Chandler implies that the world of 'logic-and-deduction' detective fiction is not the place in which most readers live. But nor is it really a world inhabited by the armchair detective. Strictly speaking, he is the only kind of detective who 'places the world under investigation'. He effectively freezes it, making it static, fixing it in time and space, in the way that a modern CSI (Crime Scene Investigator) 'secures' a crime scene. The literary theorist Tzvetan

A classic exterior: Harry Angel traverses the 'mean streets' in *Angel Heart*.

Todorov once remarked that 'we cannot imagine Hercule Poirot or Philo Vance threatened by some danger, attacked, wounded, even killed'.[14] The world investigated by the armchair detective is a static one, and he is able to remain detached from it.

By contrast, the world faced by the private eye is one which resists all attempts to place it under arrest. It is constantly moving and mutating as the detective passes through it; it is full of the potential for him to be harmed. Todorov called the kind of detective novel perfected by Hammett and Chandler 'the story of the vulnerable detective', noting that its 'chief feature is that the detective loses his immunity, gets beaten up, badly hurt, constantly risks his life, in short, he is integrated into the universe of the other characters, instead of being an independent observer as the reader is'.[15] The private eye remains at the mercy of the world he investigates.

The difference between the logic-and-deduction form of detective fiction and the hard-boiled variety is therefore the difference between a suspended world and a world of suspense. This distinction in itself offers a good reason why the latter kind should have proved dominant in cinema. A form in which the action is placed 'offstage' in favour of intellectual deliberations and discussions is obviously less cinematic. This is why the most successful cinematic uses of the whodunnit template, the Agatha Christie adaptations of the 1970s (for example, *Murder on the Orient Express*, 1974, and *Death on the Nile*, 1978), attempt to inject suspense into the otherwise plodding and undramatic 'story of the investigation' (Todorov) by illustrating those moments in which the viewer is invited to indulge in conjecture. Suspects' memories of the night of the crime and the hypotheses of the detective are acted out in scenes in which characters creep around in the dark, attack one another, or meet in secret.

The difference also means that while both forms involve placing a world under scrutiny, only in hard-boiled fiction and film noir does the private detective actually *enter* this world. He travels through it, illuminating the illicit and criminal activity going on in its private spaces. If he attempts to retreat into his office or private apartment, the world will follow him in and draw him out again. Remaining detached is not an option; all he can do is be ready for what the world might throw at him. As Easy Rawlins, the private eye in *Devil in a Blue Dress*, puts it: 'Step out your door in the morning, you're already in trouble. Just a matter of whether you're mixed up at the top of that trouble or not, that's all.' Where the classic armchair sleuth looks at the world logically, rationally, and exercises his cognitive functions to make sense of it, the private eye is compelled to explore deeper into it, living by his wits and emotions rather than relying on his ratiocinative faculties. Without the detached overview of his armchair counterpart, the private eye is more suited to exposing this world than explaining it.

Prowling:
*Out of the
Past.*

Snooping: *Kiss Me Deadly.*

The 'Homeless' Detective: Private Eye Films and the Romance

The armchair has no relevance to the world of the private eye –
and not just because it also functions as a metonym for a genteel,
leisured class to which only the European or Anglo-American
amateur detective belongs. The American detective needs to work

to remain financially independent, and neither his apartment nor his office (in which he is often threatened or even beaten up, as in *The Maltese Falcon*) provides the kind of safe haven for the solution of any mystery. He is a symbolically homeless figure, continually on the move, passing from one space to another as the case unfolds. Solving the crime is seldom his goal, for very often it is unclear what exactly 'the crime' is. Private eye stories usually begin with a mystery rather than a crime – most commonly a person who has gone missing – and his attempts to unravel it lead the detective to discover a much more complex mystery which points to hitherto occluded criminal activity. The initial case functions as a lure, a way of getting the private eye to leave the safety of his office.

Without an armchair to retreat to, the private eye would obviously seem to descend more directly from the nineteenth-century *flâneur* than Sherlock Holmes or even Dupin (who is largely sedentary). Even though the mean streets of his environment pose a continued threat to him, he remains relatively comfortable there, 'not afraid' of them, to use Chandler's phrase.[16] Though primarily shot in interiors, Huston's film of *The Maltese Falcon* depicts Spade as a highly mobile figure: we see him moving through a range of locations, from the streets of San Francisco to the hotels where the suspects have taken rooms, often leaving one place with a 'wolfish grin' on his face to move to another.[17] The impression is that he moves easily, confidently, through this world. Like the *flâneur*, Spade's apparent ability to access all areas of the urban environment at all times, night and day, would seem to make him ideally positioned to impose an overall, unifying vision on the disparate puzzle elements of the intrigue in which he is involved.

One of the distinguishing characteristics of the *flâneur* was his ability to turn the thoroughfares of the modern city 'into an interior', so he was 'as much at home in that street as he would be in his study'.[18] The private eye retains this capacity in noir. Without a stable home himself, he is nonetheless 'at home' in the streets – even though the fact that they are 'mean streets' makes this idea of 'home' something far removed from the safe haven of a domestic sphere.

The idea of the private eye as homeless wanderer points to other possible literary roots of the private eye movie, besides the *flâneur*. He might be considered a parodic descendent of the epic hero Odysseus, whose attempts to return home are continually disrupted by a series of adventures which involve either being invited into the homes of those he encounters or refused entry to them. Any comparison would be ironic because the seediness of the modern city and the detective's moral ambivalence are a long way from the epic hero and his world. There is a valid comparison to be made between the private eye story and the episodic, 'picaresque' narrative which dates back to sixteenth-century Spain, and which tells of a rogueish lower-class hero journeying through a corrupt world, living by his wits.[19] The puritanical version of this narrative (for example, in John Bunyan's *The Pilgrim's Progress*, 1678) has been used to illuminate the familiar plot development in which 'the lone investigating hero's pursuit of the criminal leads him into a descent into the underside of city life . . . where each door that is opened displays a tableau representing one further aspect of the city's decadence and corruption'.[20]

The private eye story most obviously descends, however, from another ancient narrative form: the romance. This stretches back to antiquity, to the chivalric romances involving King Arthur, such as the fourteenth-century story, *Sir Gawain and the Green Knight*, but has remained a remarkably prevalent form in modern fiction and film. Recent examples would include the novels of Haruki Murakami or the films of Steve Martin. The romantic form helps us understand how the private eye movie works. The literary critic Northrop Frye described the hero of romance as moving 'in a world in which the ordinary laws of nature are slightly suspended'.[21] This applies even to the 'low-mimetic' mode of romance, where the hero may be 'superior in degree but not in kind' to other people.[22] Martin Rubin has used Frye's ideas to suggest that the modern narrative form, the thriller, is a descendent of romance, only one 'lifted out of the romantic realm'. Rather than set in enchanted forests or castles as romance once was, the backdrop of the thriller is a recognizable modern urban world which becomes transformed into something extraordinary and dangerous by the experience the hero undergoes.[23]

This is what happens in the private eye thriller, its hero remaining 'one of us', despite his morality and bravery. What typifies romance narrative, according to Frye, is that unlike the novel, which attempts to utilize a story for a particular end (in order to explore a character type or a society or a period in history), it is uninterested in probability and delights instead in sheer patterning and repetition; it revels in *story*, in other words.

Again this strikes a chord with the convoluted plots of most private eye movies. Typically they begin with the hero being given what seems a relatively straightforward task, usually to find a missing person. But the simple job quickly spirals into a labyrinthine quest. Each satisfactorily completed task is immediately replaced by another, without the detective ever becoming aware of the overall picture until the end, when it dawns on him that the truth is uncomfortably close to home. *Harper*, for example, starts with the private eye being despatched on his quest by his client Mrs Sampson with the words 'I simply want you to find him [her missing husband] and tell me which female he's with'. In reality this means entering a world which escapes the eye of most Californians, a world of seedy bars, bohemian retreats, and private apartments, and encountering mysterious and dangerous people along the way. In the end, the trail leads him back to none other than his own close friend, Albert Graves.

The romance narrative is in fact used self-conciously in private eye movies as an ironic comment on the impossibility of these men functioning as 'knights' in their world. *The Big Sleep* has been described as 'anti-romance',[24] as taking 'the ironic form of an unnecessary journey'.[25] Marlowe ends up recognizing that the arch-criminal he has been chasing is the very girl, the wayward Carmen Sternwood, whom he had originally been hired to protect, and whom he actually had, literally, in his grasp in the opening scene when she fainted in his arms. The quest element of private eye films has been linked, by critics interested in the sexual politics of film noir, with the protagonist's need to prove and assert his potency. This is usually achieved through the conquest of a woman (usually the femme fatale) whose sexual allure and mendacity diverts him from the pursuit of knowledge.[26] There may be some truth in this, but the quest theme really operates on a wider level, depicting the private eye as an anachronistic knight figure trying to uphold the values of goodness in a corrupt world.

For all his admiration of the realism of hard-boiled fiction, Raymond Chandler was conscious of the comparison between the private eye and the flawed hero of the romance, and deliberately included allusions to medieval romance in his novels. The title of *The Lady in the Lake* (1943) is drawn from Arthurian legend. His first novel, *The Big Sleep* (1939), is full of symbols (a stained-glass window in the Sternwoods' house, on which a knight is trying to rescue a naked damsel, a chess problem which involves moving a knight, and so on) which characterize Marlowe as ironic knight-errant existing in a world incompatible with 'courtly' values.[27]

Similar romance references recur throughout the private eye tradition. In *The Narrow Margin*, 'Mrs Neall', the gangster's wife being protected by the detective Walter Brown, tells him: 'Relax,

Percy, your shield's untarnished . . . I wouldn't want any of that nobility to rub off on me.' The reference here is to Sir Percivale, the knight who was allowed to see the Holy Grail. Brown's quest is to protect a damsel in distress who is in fact – true to the logic of romance – masquerading as something she is not. She is really an undercover police officer with the Internal Affairs Division, and this means that, like the Arthurian knights undergoing a spiritual trial, he is being tested in the face of the repeated temptations to bribery offered him by the gangsters in pursuit. When he tells the real Mrs Neall, 'I never took a bribe in my life', she replies: 'Maybe your price was never met.' The ideals of chivalric romance are never endorsed by private eye movies, only suggested as a distant possibility. In reality – in noir – there is a narrow margin between nobility and corruption, and (as we shall see in chapter Four) a thin line separating professional duty and private desire.

'Backed Up in a Dark Corner': The Existential Engagement of the Private Eye

The thin line between the professional and the personal is one of the main factors which separate the noir private eye from the armchair detective, and which shapes the kind of narrative in which he features. The difference is clear as we compare the openings to each kind of detective story, according to Slavoj Žižek. Both logic-and-deduction and hard-boiled fiction begin in a similar way, he argues. The detective is lured into the case by a client who confronts him with a seductive scenario (a story of a crime, a missing person, or the discovery of a mysterious object, for example) which captures his interest before turning out to be a lie or a misinterpretation. Yet only the armchair detective offers a 'rational explanation' which breaks the spell. By contrast, the private eye quickly loses the distance required to analyze the false scene and dispel its charm; he becomes an active hero confronted with a chaotic, corrupt world, the more he intervenes in it, the more involved in its wicked ways he becomes . . . What looked at first like an easy job turns into an intricate game of criss-cross, and all his effort is directed toward clarifying the contours of the trap into which he has fallen. The 'truth' at which he attempts to arrive is not just a challenge to his reason but concerns him ethically and often painfully.[28]

Žižek thinks the detective's existential engagement is the crucial element of noir detective fiction. It explains why hard-boiled novels tend mostly to be narrated in the first person, unlike the classical detective stories of Doyle or Agatha Christie, which are narrated by the detective's companion or 'sidekick'. The first-person perspective tends to rule out an objective, detached viewpoint. It can also explain why – as the 'private eye' heroine of Thomas Pynchon's novel *The Crying of Lot 49* (1963) puts it – 'the private eye sooner or later has to get beat up on'.[29] The 'masochism' of the hard-boiled/noir template is striking,[30] and part and parcel of the viewing experience of private eye films is watching painfully violent scenes in which the private detective is beaten up (for example, in *Murder, My Sweet*, *The Lady in the Lake*, *Kiss Me Deadly*, *Harper*, *Chinatown*, *Brick* and *Manorama: Six Feet Under*, to name but a few). Again, this masochism might be considered a component of the masculine ideal promoted by American crime fiction.[31] But it also underlines the deeply personal connection between the private eye and the object of his investigation, and his inability to remain detached. He is trapped by his personal investment in a case.

This trap also explains the logic behind the detective's fee in the private eye movie. Žižek remarks that 'the hard-boiled

The dishelleved detective: a roughed-up Marlowe in *Murder, My Sweet*.

Beaten for playing detective (*Manorama*).

The masochism of Marlowe: *The Big Sleep*.

detective as a rule disdains money and solves his cases with the personal commitment of somebody fulfilling an ethical mission',[32] but he overlooks the importance of 'advance payment' as a retainer fee. In *Devil in a Blue Dress*, Easy Rawlins is first sucked in to private eye work by a crook, Albright, who gives him an advance payment of $100 to gain information about a woman, the aptly named Daphne Monet – a sum that seems surprisingly generous for a relatively simple task. But the fee ensures he cannot get out of the contract – at least not without paying it back in kind. As the film shows, private eye work involves being asked to do a series of discrete tasks, straightforward enough in themselves, one leading to another, always involving advance payment. Yet these combine to form a much more complex and dangerous case. By the time the detective realizes this, he is in too deep to escape.

The existential engagement of the private eye explains – or at least makes perfectly appropriate – two characteristic features of the plots of noir detective movies. Firstly, there is the circular effect produced by the detective's inability to divorce his own interests from the case he investigates, or to put himself out of the picture. His attempts to 'look outward' and move away from his personal investment in his job only lead him back to himself. *Out of the Past*, for example, tells the story of a former private detective who had succumbed to the temptation of corruption in his previous career, but is unable to go straight because the personal connection that obscured his professional duty in the first place – namely his love for a gangster's girlfriend – remains active and comes 'out of the past' to lead him into even more trouble and eventually death. Secondly, there is the fondness for complex, convoluted plots which create a 'maze' in which the detective gets lost[33] – a feature acknowledged in *The Lady in the Lake* by Marlowe's reference to 'Hansel and Gretel': 'I read a story once, how a detective carried rice in his pocket. He walked along – he distributed it, kernel for kernel.'

In fact, Chandler's novels, and the films based on his fiction (despite their efforts to simplify and clarify the stories), were notorious for this labyrinthine approach to plotting. There is a much-quoted and possibly apocryphal story of how Howard Hawks, puzzled by the plot while directing *The Big Sleep*, sent a telegram to Chandler to ask if the character Owen Taylor had been murdered and, if so, who was the killer. Chandler is said to have sent one back, saying 'Damned if I know!'[34] Accidental or not, the effect of complex narratives like those of *The Big Sleep* and *The Lady in the Lake* is quite appropriate, for it shifts the emphasis of the films on to the detective's experiences while lost in the labyrinth, rather than on 'the facts' of the investigation, as it would be in the logic-and-deduction detective story. *Murder, My Sweet*, an adaptation of Chandler's *Farewell, My Lovely*, is an exemplary noir private eye film, but almost the equal of Kafka's *The Trial* (1926) in the absurdity of the situation the protagonist faces. Marlowe is offered money by one person to take on the case, then money by another to drop it – without ever really understanding what is going on.

The labyrinthine element suggests that, as well as the world in which the private eye movie is set – its version of San Francisco, or Los Angeles, for example – the private detective is imprisoned in another 'world': the narrative of the film itself. Small wonder that the idea of noir as a metaphorical 'place' as much as a set of cinematic conventions has appealed to critics. Psychoanalytic theorists such as Žižek and Joan Copjec, for example, often refer to the 'noir universe' in their discussions.[35] While obviously less specific than a more technical term like 'genre', this word accurately conveys the sense of entering a characteristic world each time a viewer watches a film noir – as different as each example is from each other, and as hard as it is to come up with a definitive list of noir features.

Many noir films make this explicit by choosing titles which figure as metaphorical or metonymic references to places of desolation and desperation: *Scarlet Street*, *Dark Passage* (1947), *The Naked City* (1948), *In a Lonely Place* (1950), *Night and the City* (1950). In *The Dark Corner*, a private eye, Bradford Galt, finds himself stuck in a compulsion to repeat. Trying to begin a new life after being framed by his business partner, Jardine, and jailed for manslaughter, he is framed again by the art dealer Cathcart for Jardine's murder. For all of the film's vivid locations – in particular the high society art world, the ballrooms and luxury apartments inhabited by Cathcart and Jardine – the most important one is the eponymous imaginary space where Galt loses all his bearings: 'There goes my last lead. I feel all dead inside. I'm backed up in a dark corner, and I don't know who's hitting me.'

The World of Chinatown

Perhaps the most evocative metaphorical location in private eye movies is the eponymous *Chinatown*. As one of the second wave movies I discussed in chapter One, in which the original noir private eye is recast as an alienated, impotent figure, this film depicts its detective, Jake Gittes, becoming more and more lost in the labyrinth he has entered. The film's title refers most straightforwardly to a real district in Los Angeles – the place where Gittes cut his teeth as a detective, working for the police alongside his adversary in the movie, Lou Escobar, in what were obviously extremely challenging circumstances. Both have ostensibly got 'out of Chinatown'. But for some reason Gittes is still haunted by it. All we know about his experiences there – indeed the only detail we know about his past other than the fact he worked for the police – is that he once tried to keep a woman he cared for from being hurt, but ended up hurting her again. Although this is back story, it is also premonition, for it is precisely what happens in the film itself; in this respect, *Chinatown*'s plot is a repetition of a repetition-compulsion. Gittes tries to protect Evelyn Mulwray from her brutal incestuous father, Noah Cross, and also becomes emotionally involved with her. Yet, precisely because of how deeply he engages with the world he is investigating, he ends up driving her to her death.

The obscure implication is that this kind of inevitable, repetitive pattern is typical of what happens in Chinatown. Yet once we accept this, it means that any reference to the real location in the film becomes replaced by a metaphorical 'Chinatown' which stands as the dwelling place of impenetrable mysteries. When Cross warns Gittes, 'You may think you know what you're dealing with, but, believe me, you don't', and asks him why he is laughing, Gittes replies, 'It's what the District Attorney used to tell me in Chinatown.' Then when Evelyn asks why he finds it hard to talk about his work in Chinatown he replies, that it is because 'you can't always tell what's goin' on – like with you'. Despite his escape

Jake Gittes in *Chinatown*: 'branded' because of what he knows (or doesn't).

'Forget it Jake. It's Chinatown' (*Chinatown*).

from the *real* Chinatown, this case has returned him to its meta-phorical counterpart, the place where he cannot figure out what is going on. And of course, with ominous inevitability, Gittes, Evelyn and Katharine all find themselves in the real Chinatown for the final scene, ostensibly because this is where, at the home of Evelyn's Chinese butler, they can lie low. But, just as inevitably, Cross is in Chinatown too. Evelyn shoots him in the arm and then drives away from the police, forcing Loach – ironically a man in the employ of Gittes, not the police, as if to emphasize Gittes's culpability – to fire a fatal shot at her car from behind. In the famous last line of the movie, the second of Gittes's operatives, Walsh, advises him to 'Forget it, Jake. It's Chinatown'.

As this remark suggests, Chinatown cannot be understood, it can only be written off as a dangerous, labyrinthine space, a world of private dramas and secrets which damage those who try to plot their way through it. We might suggest that it is nothing less than the noir universe itself, a place where one attempts – to recall Auster's metaphor in *City of Glass* – to look outwards into the world but finds oneself looking at a distorted picture which one can only half-interpret and which ultimately reflects back on oneself.

'Proving is Not My Job': The Private Eye's 'Partial Vision'

Chinatown – a film all about the inability to see what is staring one in the face – depicts a detective who is powerless to do anything about what he uncovers, namely the dual-pronged 'sins of the fathers' conspiracy, where deep-rooted corruption at the heart of the Los Angeles government is paralleled by an incestuous relationship between father and daughter. So the ending is bleak, unremitting, as Jake looks upon a death which he himself has caused and also tries to come to terms with the awful secret he has uncovered. As he is led away by the police, he – like the viewer – is left with an excess of information with which neither can do anything except acknowledge the darkness of human nature and try to forget about it.

One could not imagine a detective story more at odds with those classic logic-and-deduction examples which glorify cognition. In fact, *Chinatown* resists any real closure. In the face of the awful knowledge he has gained, death would be a relief for Gittes, but this is denied him. This is a theme which runs through noir. It is what the title *The Big Sleep* refers to (even though the passage appears nowhere in the film's dialogue):

> What did it matter where you lay once you were dead? In a dirty sump or in a marble tower on top of a high hill? You were dead, you were sleeping the big sleep, you were not bothered by things like that. Oil and water were the same as wind and air to you. You just slept the big sleep, not caring about the nastiness of how you died or where you fell. Me, I was part of the nastiness now. Far more a part of it than Rusty Regan was. But the old man didn't have to be. He could lie quiet in his canopied bed, with his bloodless hands folded on the sheet, waiting. His heart was

a brief, uncertain murmur. His thoughts were as grey as ashes. And in a little while, he too, like Rusty Regan, would be sleeping the big sleep.[36]

Unlike other characters – the crook Rusty Regan, the troubled father General Sternwood ('the old man') – Marlowe, the narrator, is still in possession of knowledge when it is all over. The big sleep may be death, but it is a comfort. The implication is that there is something worse than death: that is, paradoxically, being alive and 'part of the nastiness'. Marlowe is unable finally to bring the villains to justice. Worse, he is in possession of the kind of knowledge he wishes he didn't have.[37]

Knowledge does not bring satisfactory closure in noir, and the finality of death is often denied the possessor of knowledge. The sense of dissatisfaction which hangs over these endings is typical of the private eye movie, and not just in the downbeat neo-modernist second wave. Facts may be known, but the films usually deny us a concrete explanation for what has happened, in the manner of logic-and-deduction detective fiction. Cinematic private eyes, whether they are Chandleresque detectives like Marlowe or Jake Gittes, or more everyday, jobbing detectives such as Brown in *The Narrow Margin* or Galt in *The Dark Corner*, gain some kind of insight into the mystery which surrounds them, but are rarely able to tie up the ends and produce an authoritative overall narrative in the manner of Dupin, Sherlock Holmes or Hercule Poirot. At the end the case either remains unsolved, with no one being brought to justice (*Brick*), is solved problematically (as in *The Maltese Falcon* or *The Big Sleep*), or the conclusion is so saccharine that it seems ironic (as in *The Narrow Margin* and *The Lady in the Lake*, both of which conclude with an unconvincingly harmonious union between detective and female accomplice).

The most ironic of all is *Kiss Me Deadly*. The original mafia conspiracy which drives Mickey Spillane's original 1952 novel is, in the film, transposed into an outrageous apocalyptic Cold War science-fiction plot involving a box of radioactive material. Velda, Hammer's secretary, tries to fathom who is behind the conspiracy, and asks the rhetorical question: 'Who are "they"? They are the nameless ones who kill people for the great whatsit. Does it exist? Who cares? Everyone everywhere is so involved in a fruitless search – for what?'

The metaphor usually used to convey this sidelining of the cognitive function is blindness. Private eye films are fascinated to the point of obsession with the visual regime, and more specifically, the eyes. Examples include Jeffrey peeking through the closet in *Blue Velvet*; Dorothy's and Frank's refrain 'don't look at me!' in the same film; the emphasis on the iris in *Blade Runner*'s Voight-Kampff test, designed to measure emotional empathy; or the glaring, devilish eyes of Louis Cyphre in *Angel Heart*. There is also a mild but distinctive fetishizing of the technology of vision, especially the camera (as we can see in the film *Manorama: Six Feet Under*), the binoculars (as in *Chinatown*) or video surveillance (as in *The Eye of the Beholder* and *8mm*, both 1999). Photographic evidence – either trustworthy or not – is central to the plots of numerous private eye movies: *Chinatown*, *Blade Runner*, *Mortelle Randonnée* (1983), *Blood Simple*. But most significant are moments when the detective cannot see.

Murder, My Sweet begins and ends with Marlowe literally unable to see what has happened. The story of the film is book-ended by two scenes in which he tells the police the whole story – the story told in flashbacks is what constitutes the film. He has a bandage over his eyes because, as we learn from the final show-down, he has tried to prevent one man shooting another only for the gun to go off beside his face and burn his eyes. His blindness

The blinded private eye: *Murder, My Sweet.*

means he is genuinely in the dark about how the story has ended, even though he has been present all along. 'That's all I know', he protests to the sceptical police who interrogate him. Like Gittes, he is unable to see what has been in front of his eyes until the very end – and he too comes to the recognition too late to prevent the deaths of both Grayle and Malloy. The difference is that Marlowe's blindness is signified literally.

The emphasis on vision is quite appropriate for a medium, film, that involves looking. But it is more than simply a cinematic way of conveying the breakdown of the cognitive process. Cognition is an intellectual activity which depends on the rational faculties. Seeing, witnessing, overlooking, watching, are all – though they assist in the cognitive process (by prompting intuition or leading to perception) – more instinctive, visceral activities than reasoning, less easy to control or direct. While what a detective sees is closely linked to what he knows, interpretation is less the concern in private eye movies than spectacle.

There is of course always a case, a plot, and this, by and large, becomes clear at the end. By then we may be able to conclude that people are greedy, selfish, or have been conditioned to be this way by some traumatic episode in the past. But still the mystery of the other person, their intimate self, remains. My contention is that the function of the private eye in detective cinema is less to interpret than to *unveil* private worlds and place them 'on display' for others' eyes (primarily the viewer). In *Harper*, Graves warns the detective that all the evidence he has gathered together is 'pretty insubstantial', only for Harper to reply that 'proving is not my job'. What his job does involve is *uncovering* the bits and pieces of the narrative, laying them bare for others' eyes. Rather than providing a definitive interpretation – the endpoint towards which the armchair detective story is directed – the private eye roams from one place to another, exposing the private spaces of other people, and the secret behaviour which has been acted out within these spaces.

The emphasis on vision in the examples above also shows what is particular about the anti-cognitive emphasis which runs through hard-boiled fiction, when it comes to cinema. We see what the detective sees, usually when and how he sees it. Prose fiction offers an equivalent experience: the first-person perspective favoured by the hard-boiled novel means its world is always filtered through the consciousness of the detective-narrator; we never inhabit it 'objectively'. In his remarks on hard-boiled detective fiction Todorov notes that the 'vulnerable detective's' integration into the same universe as the other characters means that he cannot be 'an independent observer' like the reader.[38] Yet this statement does not apply to the private eye film. The viewer may be 'independent' in that he or she is not personally involved in the world depicted on screen, and can draw his or her own conclusions about this world.

Yet the cinematic viewer is in fact a *dependent* viewer in a way the reader of prose fiction is not: when watching a film, we depend on the movement of the camera for what we can see and know about the world of a movie.

This dependence is especially marked in the movie thriller, which, as the film theorist Pascal Bonitzer has argued, creates a 'labyrinthine' structure. It does this not only through its depiction of maze-like spaces and its suspenseful plotting which keeps the viewers guessing as to what is likely to confront them around the next 'corner'. The 'labyrinth' is created by its camera-work, which continually withholds and reveals what is outside the immediate field of vision.[39] A definitive characteristic of cinema, according to André Bazin,[40] is the constant interplay between on-screen and off-screen spaces sustained by the point of view continually moving. A thriller turns what is depicted on screen and what we apprehend 'off-screen' into a kind of 'labyrinth' for the eye. Watching a thriller is like walking through a maze, heart pounding and breathing heavily in anticipation of what lies ahead.

The private eye movie is an exemplary form of movie thriller. It favours labyrinthine locations, such as the Los Angeles Marlowe traverses in *The Big Sleep*, which itself includes a range of maze-like places:

> General Sternwood's hothouse (with its spokelike layout of different chambers and passages branching off a central entrance area), the casino parking-lot (where . . . Marlowe lies in wait for a would-be thief) and the Fulwider office building (where Marlowe witnesses a murder through a zigzag of cracked doorways and frosted-glass windows).[41]

It intensifies the experience of being in a labyrinth through its cinematic strategy of withholding and revealing what is round

Around the corner . . . : the 'labyrinthine' *The Big Sleep*.

Watching: *Eye of the Beholder*.

The labyrinthine staircase (*Kiss Me Deadly*).

the corner, restricting and expanding the point of view. The result is not only continual suspense. It also has the effect of revealing the world the detective has entered and stimulating our curiousity about it in a way which cannot be replicated in any other medium. The private eye enters the private spaces of other people, which contain secrets both particular and universal (the lives of the rich versus the lives of the poor, for example) and which are immediately important to the case (such as stories of conspiracy, blackmail and murder).

'Partial vision', to use Bonitzer's phrase, typifies not just the movie thriller but the detective-work of the private eye – and I use this term again here not simply to refer to the profession it denotes, private investigation, but the eye which views privately, which only sees parts of the entire field of vision, never the whole. The private eye's partial vision is one reason why the investigation in detective movies involves exposing and unveiling – in some cases, linking (as we shall see) – aspects of a world and a narrative rather than developing a total overview of the entire story. His vision is also partial in the sense that it is not necessarily objective nor even benign, but tainted by his own desire. The second two chapters of this book will consider in more depth the effects of the private eye's partial vision by examining the actual spaces of private eye thrillers.

The jobbing detective: *The Narrow Margin*.

3

Working: *The Private Eye and the Spaces of Noir*

. . . all I can do, Albert, is just do the dirty job all the way down the line. – *Harper*

Noir is a claustrophobic space, a labyrinth of mean streets, a dark corner, a distorted Chinatown: a byword for locations where contemporary anxieties find expression but not dissolution. Raymond Borde and Étienne Chaumeton, two of the early French critics who 'invented' noir, claimed that

> The noir film is black for us, that is, specifically for the Western and American moviegoers of the 1950s. It exists in response to a certain mood at large in this particular time and place. Accordingly one who seeks the root of this 'style' must think in terms of an affected and possibly ephemeral reaction to a moment in history.[1]

Noir might be thought of as a place in which whatever is 'black for us', whatever troubles us, whatever we cannot resolve either in our personal lives or in our historical moment, is played out. Yet the nature of cinema means the metaphorical noir 'universe' these films take us into is always made up of real places, either specific locations or plausible, studio-created, versions of towns and cities in the United States and the kind of places we might reasonably expect to have found there. Examples are the docks in San Francisco in *The Maltese Falcon*, the shabby apartment block in Chicago where the dramatic opening of *The Narrow Margin* is set, or the 'labyrinthine' Los Angeles in *The Big Sleep*.

Acknowledging the peculiar, evocative locations of noir has been a mainstay of critical studies from the outset.[2] But it is surprising that only comparatively recently have critics considered noir locations as more than merely 'setting', that is, the backdrop to more important matters of plot and character, or a canvas for stylistic effects. Two of these, Vivian Sobchack and Joan Copjec, have argued that alongside its other characteristic features (dark tone, distorted vision, urban setting, and so on) noir specialized in the depiction of curiously nondescript, empty places – empty, that is, because either actually depopulated or symbolically devoid of personality.[3] They describe the 'characteristic architecture' of film noir as either 'uninhabited spaces' – 'office buildings late at night, in the early hours of the morning; abandoned warehouses; hotels mysteriously untrafficked; eerily empty corridors . . .'[4] – or places which typically 'resist individual particularity and are made for transients and transcience':[5] hotel rooms, boarding-house rooms, diners, bars, hotel lobbies, cocktail lounges, roadhouses, nightclubs, bus and railway stations. None of these are what might be considered 'normal' – or what Sobchack calls 'culturally normative' – domestic spaces.

While seemingly obvious, Copjec's and Sobchack's emphasis on the locations of noir manage simultaneously to reinforce the metaphorical assertions repeated by generations of critics (that noir depicts a lonely, pessimistic, urban world) by rigorous attention to what the films actually contain, and also to defamiliarize a kind of film in danger of losing its capacity to surprise *because* of this repeated critical mantra. This chapter considers the effect these spaces have on 'detective noir' in both the classic period and the

Work versus home in *The Narrow Margin*.

second wave of private eye movies. It is perhaps more accurate to say that its concern is with the effect the *detective* has on these typical noir spaces. He exposes them for what they are, and at times is able to change them. As he passes through them, we realize that as much as the noir detective movie is about the excesses and crimes of the modern world, it is also, perhaps surprisingly, about two more mundane features of modern existence: work and home.

Part I: 'Lounge Time' in Classic Noir

Noir favours empty places, Sobchack argues, because post-war American life is characterized both by a longing for a nourishing, intimate and secure home, and by the acceptance that this home has been forever lost to its citizens because of the traumatic upheavals of the Second World War. The classic noir era coincides with upheavals in the way many Americans lived which led to

'Lounge' space: *Kiss Me Deadly*.

concerns about what 'home' signified in both local and national senses of the term. The period after the Second World War saw a large-scale migration (often described as the 'white flight') from increasingly overcrowded cities to new racially homogenous suburban zones on the outskirts of cities. The move generated not simply concerns about the emptiness or meaninglessness of existence in soulless, uniform examples of suburban 'tract' housing, but a fear about urban degeneration. This anxiety about home is discernible in a movie like *It's a Wonderful Life* (1946), which sets its *Christmas Carol*-like morality tale against the backdrop of the housing shortages created by migration and the 'baby boom', or in John Cheever's prose fiction of the 1950s, which depicts the mundane lives of those who live in the new suburbs. But Sobchack contends that it is expressed most powerfully in film noir.

The various locations she identifies, the lounge bars and hotel rooms, and so on, figure as 'units' which, linked together, convey the message that the need for a 'home front' – not simply the domestic support for the war effort, but a cosy, intimate, nourishing community space yearned for by those affected by the war – is 'broken'.[6] There are houses in noir, Sobchack notes, but 'hardly any homes'. Homes appear 'only in glimpses – as something lost or something fragile and threatened'. This is true even of 'the cold interiors of the houses of the rich and corrupt' that feature in movies such as *Laura*, *The Killers* and *The Dark Corner*, places which advertise the fact that 'money buys interior decoration and fine art but no warmth, no nurturance'.[7] Noir is a world where there is no space for the cycles and rituals of the family: no weddings, no births, no family meals. Children rarely appear, women are seldom mothers, and men almost never fathers. Of course there are many women, but they are not involved in cooking or raising a family, and 'their sexuality remains undisciplined'.

While the emphasis is on what Sobchack calls 'lounge time', this should not be confused with a keen appetite for leisure. Instead, the noir world is pervaded by 'restlessness', 'a lack of occupation'. It is not a place for work: 'Very few men (or women) can be said to labor in film noir. Most of them wait, hang on and hang around, making plans that go up in the smoke of a torch song or too many stubbed-out cigarettes.'[8] Indeed, nothing is 'normal' or innocent in noir, not even death; it is always murder or suicide. Rather than love we have sexual attraction. Marriage is depicted in some films, but only as something to be got out of. The spaces of noir are populated by appropriately 'transient' characters: they are restless, dispossessed, lacking in roots and occupation. There is no evidence of traditional social networks or places (such as the Bailey Building and Loan Association in *It's a Wonderful Life*). Instead people in noir meet by chance and find nothing, no sense of social cohesion or obligation, to prevent them acting impulsively and behaving in ways which are 'socially problematic, ambiguous, and dangerous'.[9]

Sobchack's description of the spaces of noir is instantly compelling. It is obvious, even watching a handful of film noirs,

'Lounge' space: *The Big Sleep*.

that there is something strange and alienating about the places we are shown. In Fritz Lang's *Scarlet Street*, for example, a prostitute and her pimp (or at least that is what we think they are, as their professions can only be implied because of the need to observe the Hays Code)[10] rent an expensive apartment with the potential to be used as an art studio – a necessary detail in their plan to blackmail a painter. As they are shown around the empty, lavishly decorated top-floor apartment, she pretends unconvincingly to be an artist, while he makes negative statements like, 'Where's the bedroom?' and 'I don't like the wallpaper'. We cut to a scene shortly after they have moved in, and the place is a mess. They have made no real effort to furnish it beyond putting in basic items such as a bed and armchairs: the bookshelves are still empty, cigarettes, cushions and clothes are strewn over the floor. The only personal touches are so weird they have an estranging effect:

there are stuffed animals on the mantelpiece and by the bed. At the centre of the film is the relationship between a man and a woman. But it can only be a parody of a domestic relationship because the couple's environment seems so dysfunctional.

'Work Time': Private Eye Noir

Sobchack's theory seems immediately applicable to the private eye movie. We can see this by considering a moment of unintentional black comedy in *The Dark Corner*. The hoodlum Stauffer has made sure he kills Jardine in Galt's apartment so the detective is left as prime suspect. Galt's dwelling is a typical noir space: it is what passes for home, but it is empty, dark, moribund, devoid of anything which signifies family, domesticity or intimacy. Needing to act urgently before the crime can be pinned on them,

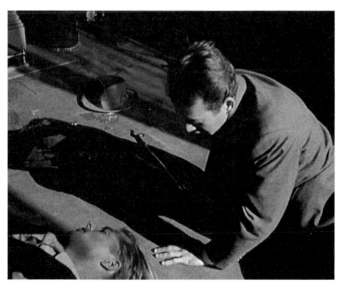

Bradford Galt (Mark Stevens) finds a dead body in his apartment: *Dark Corner*.

Galt and his secretary, Kathleen, are about to leave the apartment when Kathleen suddenly realizes that this will mean leaving Jardine's dead body there. The detective tells her not to worry: 'They only clean up once a week. The maid never cleans under the bed. That'll give me a head start.' It is clear he doesn't care enough about his home to mind a dead body lying around for a couple of days; he clearly doesn't intend to use the apartment. They flee without further ceremony to Kathleen's apartment – which is equally unhomely.

Both apartments appear to be just what they are: sets designed to look like homes, furnished with armchairs, sideboards, pictures on the wall, which all seem to have been purchased from the same warehouse and arranged by the same person, and consequently emptied of any intimate content. This is one obvious result of the shoestring priorities of b-movie production. Film noirs usually had to be shot cheaply and rapidly – often borrowing sets from other movies – and needed to convey the appropriate contexts for their characters as quickly as possible.[11] But while surely unintentional, the emphasis is nonetheless in keeping with the symbolism of the films: film noir presents us with spaces that have not 'been experienced', as the cultural theorist Gaston Bachelard might put it. Houses and apartments are actually little more than 'geometrical objects' made of brick, mortar and glass, but we humanize them, and conceive of homes as living entities, fitting spaces to accommodate the human body and soul.[12] But film noir – according to Sobchack – manages to resist such thinking. The human element is banished, and we are left merely with empty, geometrical space.

Sobchack's reading of noir helps reinforce the idea of the hard-boiled/noir private eye's symbolic 'homelessness', as if he were cast out on a quest for knowledge without being able to retreat to any safe, domestic haven. On an obvious level, the private eye comfortably conforms to her profile of the noir character. Galt in *The Dark Corner* is just as rootless and transient as countless others in film noir, detached from the traditional places and networks which give society a sense of nourishing community. His own apartment is little more than a geometrical figure, certainly nothing like a domestic or intimate space.

This is also true of Spade in *The Maltese Falcon*, the film which sets the standard for the noir private detective. Although the movie was shot on a modest budget, Huston was aware of the importance of the interiors and he constructed sets specifically designed, according to Warner's publicity department, to replicate 'real rooms and offices with real ceilings' rather than the 'familiar catwalks, blazing lights overhead'.[13] This emphasis on the interior results in a surprising effect in the film. Even though it is the vehicle for a newly mobile and fearless detective and features a

A typically claustrophobic interior in *The Maltese Falcon*.

range of exterior locations such as the San Francisco streets and waterfront, most of the key dramas in *The Maltese Falcon* are played out in private interiors. Spade pursues, encounters and interrogates the criminals in the kinds of 'lounge' places identified by Sobchack, such as Gutman's suite at the Alexandra hotel, Cairo's bedroom and the lobby in the Belvedere.

These places are as empty of private, personal, touches as the apartments in *Scarlet Street* or *The Dark Corner*. But so are the two main locations in the movie, interiors over which Huston took particular care: Spade's office, to which we are continually returned as the action continues, and the detective's own apartment. I will return to the question of the detective's office in a moment, but Spade's apartment sees no 'private' activity take place, nor is it any more intimate or personalized than Bradford Galt's. It is just somewhere he sleeps when he is not at work.

Although Spade is more heroic and mythical a figure than Bradford Galt, he is nonetheless rootless, living a transient existence, devoid of the trappings of 'cultural normativity'. On the face of it, *The Maltese Falcon* aligns with Sobchack's suggestive reading of film noir. It is a movie which, through its impersonal, non-intimate locations, its apartments, offices, hotel rooms and lobbies, and also through its ironic parody of domestic gatherings and Spade's inability to forge a properly nourishing relationship away from work, indicates that home and its connotations of intimacy, security and nourishment simply do not signify in this world.

But here we need to consider in more depth Spade's office in *The Maltese Falcon*, and what it signifies. In terms of its decor, size and furnishings, it too resembles the kind of transient rent-by-the-week space which is typical of the locations in film noir. Yet, unlike Spade's apartment, in which he does nothing but sleep and wake up, his office is the object of very personal pride. One

Spade and Archer's office in *The Maltese Falcon*.

'Take Archer off and, er, have Samuel Spade put on'.

of his first moves after his partner Miles Archer is murdered is to order his secretary Effie Perrine to 'have "Spade and Archer" taken off all the doors and windows and, er, have "Samuel Spade" put on'.

Most importantly, Spade's office is the literal embodiment of his inexorable need to work – a definitive feature of the private eye movie from classic noir to recent examples such as *Manorama Six Feet Under* or *Zodiac* (2007). John Irwin has argued that one way of making sense of the hard-boiled tradition in fiction and film is as a continual assertion of the significance of *work* in the American psyche. The private detective, he suggests, is an embodiment of the 'desire for personal freedom' which 'has been central to American identity from the outset, since the pioneers set out to own and work their own land'.[14] This is why 'a major thematic trajectory' in Hammett's and Chandler's fiction is the detective's movement 'from a salaried employee of a large private agency (the Continental Op and Spade) or of the DA's office (Marlowe) to being a self-employed, independent operator'.[15] The upward movement of the private eye reflects the fact that 'the twentieth-century urban survival of that desire for a freedom grounded on economic independence has often been the attempt to control one's own destiny, be one's own boss, by owning one's own business'.[16]

This argument is not incompatible with the 'romantic-individualist' view of the private eye as an outsider-hero. 'Being one's own boss' might figure as a shorthand metaphor for the existentialist freedom the detective is seen by some to represent. Yet a less romantic version of this argument is advanced by Marc Vernet, who argues that rather than offering a critique of the entire system, the noir detective movie is about asserting the values of the ordinary bourgeoisie and entrepreneurship, with the private eye as little more than 'a petty-bourgeois jealous of his independence, convinced of his moral worth and concerned with protecting what is, in his eyes, the exemplary value of American democracy'.[17] In my view, the importance of work in the life of the private eye is a limit to his freedom rather than something which makes it possible, even though the actual nature of his job means he is less subject to the occupational rules imposed by a boss than other professions in the capitalist system. The private eye, to paraphrase Sartre, is 'condemned to work'.

The detective's work ethic shows there is something missing in Sobchack's reading of film noir. A recurring noir location not mentioned in her litany of noir spaces is the detective's office. It too tends to be populated by transient, mysterious strangers – his clients and associates – but it remains very much the private eye's personal domain, the location for his work. It is far from a 'home from home' (Bailey in *Out of the Past* calls his office a 'cheap little rat hole'), but what it signifies still means something to him –

Working late: Galt's office in *The Dark Corner*.

everything, in fact. But what we see him doing there has a purpose lacking in the kind of exchanges we are presented with in the noir parade of lounge bars and nightclubs.

Although the private eye may be as fundamentally disaffected as the rest of the characters in noir, living in an environment which is the opposite of a conventionally private, family space, indulging in erotic encounters which are a long way from nourishing love, given to acting impulsively in ways that run counter to the norms of everyday working life, still he has a purpose and an energy which is seldom present in others. He labours continuously, forever being called from one place to another, and is rarely seen relaxing. Rather than sleeping and being woken, he is startled out of sleep by the phone or suddenly comes to in the morning – to be thrust immediately into work again. The private eye is the glaring exception to Sobchack's rule that characters seldom 'labor in film noir'. Where the restless and rootless figures she refers to simply 'lounge' around, neither working nor playing, the private eye does nothing *but* work.

Steven Marcus's question, 'Which side was [the private eye] on?', is something of a red herring. What he represents is the job itself – not even the economic independence it might lead to, but its mechanics, its procedure, the endless unquenchable need to acquire knowledge. This sense of vocation is something Spade expresses in a famous speech from Hammett's original *The Maltese Falcon* (which is, surprisingly, not there in the faithful film version). He tells Brigid that he will not save her from the police even though he could, 'because I'm a detective and expecting me to run criminals down and then let them go free is like asking a dog to catch a rabbit and let it go. It can be done . . . and sometimes it is done, but it's not the natural thing.'[18] Spade is referring to something beyond morality here, beyond even desire. As the canine comparison suggests, this is more like instinct.

We arrive here at a key difference between the hard-boiled detective and the armchair detective, who – lest we be mistaken – works relentlessly, too. Work is what enables Sherlock Holmes to keep functioning, almost like a drug. In *The Sign of Four* (1890) he tells Watson that his mind

> rebels at stagnation. Give me problems, give me work, give me the most abstruse cryptogram, or the most intricate analysis, and I am in my own proper atmosphere . . . The work itself, the pleasure of finding a field for my peculiar powers, is my highest reward.[19]

But Holmes's work is not ceaseless labour, but an exalted alternative to boredom. A poor supplement for him is the '7% solution' of cocaine towards which his 'pathological and morbid' habit is geared.[20]

Besides underlining his credentials as a rootless, transient, quintessentially noir, character, the unhomeliness of the private eye's home conveys the message that he is *always* at work. Just after Archer is killed, *The Maltese Falcon* cuts to a scene in which the phone rings in Spade's apartment, waking him up to tell him the news. It is a recurring moment in private eye movies. In *Chinatown*, when we are finally given a glimpse into Jake Gittes's home life, no sooner has he taken a shower, closed the curtains and settled down to bed than he receives two phone calls from his office, despatching him straight away to Ida Sessions's apartment. In *Farewell, My Lovely*, Marlowe returns to his office after a week's absence (during which he has been holed up in a 'dingy hotel room', 'ducking the police'), and immediately the phone rings. It suggests either that he is always at the mercy of the sudden phone call, or, worse, that the phone has been ringing constantly all the time he has been away.

Marlowe's low-rent apartment in *Farewell, My Lovely*.

Unlike Holmes, or Poe's Dupin, who can take on only the cases which interest them – as grateful as they are to have the opportunity to relieve the boredom – the noir private eye does not decide when he works: it is 'Work' itself which decides. As Marlowe puts it in *The Lady in the Lake*:

> My name is Marlowe, Philip Marlowe. Occupation: Private Eye. You know, somebody says 'follow that guy', so I follow him. Somebody says 'find that female!', so I find her. And what do I get? Ten bucks a day and expenses . . .

The case in which Mike Hammer is engaged in *Kiss Me Deadly* is not one he has chosen: it is because he just happens to be driving on the same deserted highway at night as a woman on the run from dangerous criminals. The private eye's profession has no respect for his private life. In fact, the emphasis on constant work underlines the fact that he has no private life of his own.

This is clear in early noirs such as *The Maltese Falcon*, *Murder, My Sweet* and *The Big Sleep*. Neither Spade nor Marlowe engage in any 'private' activity; no detachment from the shady world the detective is investigating is possible, there is no way he can separate his private life from his professional one. He is on screen practically the whole time, but it is almost purely to service the insatiable demands of work. The only moments which gesture towards opportunities for relaxation are the seduction scenes. Early in *The Big Sleep*, for example, when Marlowe finds his entry into Geiger's rare bookstore barred by the tall, beautiful 'gate-keeper', Agnes, he visits the pretty proprietress of the bookshop across the street. Within minutes she has closed the shop early, drawn down the blinds, removed her glasses and let her hair down, and is sharing an intimate whisky with him. Yet he is there on business, and he resumes his business straight after. It is natural to assume that this bit in the middle amounts to business as well.

A convention of the private eye tradition is the detective – as happens in *Out of the Past*, *The Narrow Margin* and *Laura*, for example – having an intimate relationship with a female client or suspect (in noir, sometimes the two categories are inseparable). In some examples (like *The Narrow Margin*) she is benign and trustworthy; more often she is manipulative, and bent on diverting him from his purpose. But in each case, she stands as the very embodiment of Work. This logic is emphasized in *The Maltese Falcon*, where the philandering Spade's other relationships are also dictated by his work. As well as his affair with the client/suspect (Brigid O'Shaughnessy), he is also seeing his secretary (Effie Perrine), and the wife of his former partner (Ida Archer). Spade's private life is full of professional relationships. In his world, as in those of other cinematic private eyes, there is no stable division

The end of *The Narrow Margin*.

between the private and professional in the realm of the private eye: the private *is* the professional.

'No Place Like Home': Noir Nostalgia

When we look at film noir as a whole, as Sobchack does, we see that it is indeed dominated by lounge spaces, inertia and 'homelessness'. But when we turn our attention specifically to the noir detective movie – a significant enough minority within the overall noir canon to alter our thoughts about it (and widely credited as the original form of film noir)[21] – we find something rather different. There is a continual contrast between lounge time and 'work time'. In the figure of the private eye the latter can intrude into the former, transforming it, animating it. Wherever the detective is, there is action and there is meaning – or at least the potential for meaning. As soon as he enters a lounge space its ambience is altered. We observe this in the many scenes in which the private eye enters bars and clubs, for example, in *The Big Heat* or in *Murder, My Sweet*, where his presence is immediately noted by at least one person already there, and often leads to some significant event, such as a conversation, a fight, or an argument.

Ultimately the depiction of 'work time' in the private eye movie does not dispel the typically noir air of dislocation and homelessness, it reinforces it. Rather than the detective's labour supporting his domestic life (which would be the conventional, bourgeois ideal), it threatens it. It is widely acknowledged that on the rare occasions when film noir sets its stories in 'traditional domestic spaces . . . the threat of violent crime [is brought] into the home'.[22] The private eye movie is no exception, as it repeatedly presents us with occasions when work – and the violent consequences of the detective's job – intrudes upon the private eye's domestic space. We can see this not simply in the inhospitable domestic environments of films such as *The Dark Corner* and *The Maltese Falcon*, which constitute the norm in detective noir, but also in the few private eye dwellings which are closer to being proper homes. We might consider, for example, Mike Hammer's apartment in *Kiss Me Deadly*, a luxurious dwelling compared to Spade's or Marlowe's, one adorned with pictures and sculptures, as well as a huge state-of-the-art answering machine fixed to the wall which he uses to screen his calls. Or we could consider the domestic harmony patiently detailed at the beginning of *The Big Heat*, when the detective Dave Bannion returns home from investigating the case of a suicide and we see him sitting at home in an armchair, reading the paper, asking his wife 'What's for dinner?', before discussing their daughter's schooling over the meal.

Yet in both cases these homes are soon intruded upon by the mundane demands of 'work' or, in *The Big Heat*, by the more catastrophic results of Bannion's job. Hammer lounges on his sofa and 'entertains' female guests in his apartment, but is also in the habit of suspiciously checking it over when he returns home, assuming it has been visited by an intruder. Bannion is subject to menacing phone calls, and then his wife is murdered by a car bomb intended for him – detonated symbolically while he is reading his daughter a bedtime story. From this point, Bannion, until then an ordinary police detective, becomes the private eye, resigning from his post, returning his badge but keeping his gun, and beginning a 'hate binge' (as a colleague calls it) aimed at getting even with the gangster, Lagana, who is responsible for the attack. The next time we see the house it is empty. Bannion has left, put his belongings into storage, and sent his daughter away for safety. He is no longer father or husband, and the house is no longer a home. It is only at this point, as Sobchack notes,[23]

The domestic detective: *The Big Heat*.

Hammer returns home suspiciously: *Kiss Me Deadly*.

that the film becomes a film noir in its technical features, the scenes made shadowy and dingy with the characteristic noir lighting effects. Bannion is now out on the streets, at large in the kind of desolate, transitional spaces which typify the noir universe, seeking out suspects, and lurking in the shadows outside the hoodlums' apartments.

The Big Heat, as befits one of the post-1948 film noirs Paul Schrader once labelled as 'manic, neurotic',[24] displays the symptom at the heart of noir's anxiety about domesticity. It questions whether someone who has not worked for it in the appropriate (socially normative, 'non-noir') way, should be entitled to a private, comfortable domestic life. One of the unexplained elements in the past of the man, Duncan, whose suicide Bannion begins by investigating, is that he owned a second home which he and his wife could not have afforded simply on his salary. Mrs Duncan is accused of continuing to protect her husband's murderer, Lagana, and his criminal associate, Stone, 'for the sake of a plush life'. Bannion comments ironically when he visits her later, that in her house, 'the furniture's the same, nothing has been changed, you haven't started living "high" yet, have you?'

This kind of dishonest acquisition, living the high life as a result of corruption, is what the film challenges, setting hard-working honest domesticity against dishonest corruption. The subject fuels the key confrontation between private detective and master criminal. Bannion responds to a threatening phone call to his home by confronting Lagana in his, prompting the gangster to exclaim, outraged, 'You came here, to my home, about a murder?! . . . I'm glad to help you boys whenever I can. But I got an office for that sort of thing. This is my home, and I don't like dirt tracked into it.' In response Bannion sneers at the fact that Lagana's home is 'too elegant, too respectable, nice kids, party, painting of mom up there on the wall . . . It's only a place for a hoodlum who built this place outta twenty years of corruption

Work intrudes into home: Spade interrogated in *The Maltese Falcon*.

and murder! . . . You couldn't plant enough flowers around here to kill the smell!' The paradox is that Bannion's job means that he works hard and 'appropriately' enough to be entitled to a stable, nourishing home, but the nature of his work means that he is barred from having one. When he shows Debbie Marsh, his companion, into the sparse hotel room that he is renting after moving out of his home, she looks at the style of its interior and comments ironically, 'Say, I like this . . . early nothing!' The criminal, on the other hand, is able to preserve a properly separate domestic life without adhering to the laws of respectable society.

Dean MacCannell has suggested that 'the best way to characterize *noir* sensibility is as "false nostalgia" or "constructed nostalgia". What is produced is a sense of the loss of something that was never possessed.'[25] This certainly applies to the question of home in private eye noirs. In fact, Elisabeth Bronfen has contended that whenever Hollywood films are concerned with 'concepts of home' – which is remarkably often, as her book *Home in Hollywood* shows – they are 'inscribed by a nostalgia for an untainted sense of belonging, and the impossibility of achieving that is also the catalyst for fantasies about recuperation and healing'.[26] This, she thinks, drawing on the psychoanalytic account of subjectivity, is because cinema enables viewers to play out the unconscious narrative of 'psychic dislocation' which we all share as a result of being separated from our original 'home': our nourishing infantile union with the mother.

Noir is outside the scope of Bronfen's study, no doubt because it does the opposite to the 'devising [of] protective fictions', which is the aim of her particular object of study, Hollywood film. Yet the private eye movie suggests that film noir essentially rearranges the same coordinates as a film as strikingly different on the face of it as *The Wizard of Oz* (1939). It constructs narratives and depicts spaces which evoke a sense of dislocation and loss which prompt nostalgia (the literal meaning of 'nostalgia', which comes from the Greek, is 'home-pain').

A good example of this is Jacques Tournier's masterful noir *Out of the Past*, which tells the story of a former private eye's inability completely to renounce the profession of private detective once his past life has caught up with him. On the face of it, Bailey returns to his old line of work because he still owes something to the gangster he once double-crossed, Sterling. But really it is because he cannot fully inhabit the ordinary life he has begun, living in a small town, running a gas station and trying to live a simple life with a new, uncomplicated, girlfriend. The film is sceptical about any idea of a peaceful domestic life. This is signalled later by a romanticized memory he shares with his former lover, Kathie, about the time they spent together in a mountain resort hideaway in Bridgeport, California. 'Remember the mountains?', she asks him, wistfully. 'Higher than these and always snow on them. We should have stayed there.' The nostalgic nature of this vision, powerfully conveyed via the lush 'melancholy romanticism' of the cinematography,[27] is precisely what exposes their longing for a 'home' as futile, because it never existed in the first place.

Seeing the nostalgic image with their own eyes, viewers are not fooled for a minute into accepting it as a genuine alternative to *Out of the Past*'s claustrophobic narrative. Disbelief is also invited by other classic noirs in which private investigators enjoy moments of what seems to be normal domestic happiness. One of the ill-advised liberties taken by *The Lady in the Lake* in adapting Chandler's original novel is to show Philip Marlowe in love with his client Adrienne Fromsett, and ready to settle down, give up his job and live off the proceeds of his writing (perhaps a plausible development given Marlowe's status as narrator but nevertheless at odds with his need to be out on the mean streets). On Christmas morning she makes a pot of coffee then they listen to an appropriately hammy adaptation of *A Christmas Carol* on the radio, before chatting about their pasts. It is impossible to believe. Even in *The Dark Corner*, where Galt's and Kathleen's relationship is far more plausible, our suspicions are aroused. After escaping to her apartment, we see him sleeping there, the window open, traffic outside, while she brings in coffee. Then the milkman turns up at the door, after which they have breakfast. But it is a scene so improbably idyllic that it only serves to emphasize that noir, the world of dark corners, has no room for sunny domesticity.[28]

Such glimpses of domestic harmony must be considered in the context of post-war anxiety about home, as expressions of longing for a stable, harmonious domestic space barred to Americans by the Second World War – but which never existed in such an uncomplicated guise in the first place. Although Kathleen's

Marlowe and Adrienne Fromsett in *The Lady in the Lake*.

breakfast table seems to figure as the very opposite of the 'dark corner' in which Galt is trapped, their conversation as they eat continues to evoke this metaphorical space: 'How do you fight back, if you don't know who you're fighting?' Once again, though more subtly than a late-night telephone call, domestic space is invaded here by the insistent demands of work.

Part II: California in the Second Wave

The idea of an absent or barred home continues to haunt the second wave of noir detective movies, though their socio-historical context is naturally very different. While films such as *Harper*, *The Long Goodbye*, *Chinatown*, *Farewell, My Lovely*, *Night Moves* and *Marlowe* feature places which are outwardly quite unlike the claustrophobic interiors which characterize noir in the classic period, on closer inspection we can see that they perform a similar function.

Two main kinds of place are depicted in these films. Firstly there are the kind of seedy interiors peopled with undesirables or transients that typify classic noir and which Sobchack and Copjec detail: bars, diners, hotel rooms, lobbies, apartments and so on, places which represent blue-collar America.

Detective films of the 1960s and '70s are full of equivalent 'lounge' locations, such as the down-at-heel nightclubs where Harper meets the junky singer Betty Fraley and the overweight, alcoholic former starlet Fay Estabrook, or the store where Marlowe goes to buy catfood at the beginning of *The Long Goodbye*. Other films choose to set their narratives in the time of the original period of noir, making their films, somewhat problematically, partial nostalgic homages to the original cycle of private eye movies.

This is what both *Chinatown* and *Farewell, My Lovely* do, the latter example in particular replicating the kind of spaces we find

The club in *Klute*.

in original noir, such as Marlowe's run-down hotel apartment, the cheap hotel where Velma is holed up, and the seedy bar on the gambling ship at the climax to the film. The problem is that this gesture compromises both films' potential to convey genuine historical 'depth'. Fredric Jameson argued that, excellent as it was, *Chinatown*, set in post-Depression 1937, was essentially a 'nostalgia film', a pastiche of previous movies rather than a representation of history in itself.[29] Partly this is inevitable, for, as Dean MacConnell has argued, the actual spaces of noir, 'the kind of urban domestic space once inhabited by the poorest of the working poor', had begun to disappear after 1955 due to efforts by successive governments to remove them.[30]

A nightclub in *Harper*.

The second kind of place which dominates in the second wave films is perhaps more interesting: the grand, expansive homes of the wealthy. As well as Grayle's palatial mansion in *Farewell, My Lovely* ('The house itself wasn't much, it was smaller than Buckingham Palace, and probably had fewer windows than the Chrysler Building'), and 'The White Orchid' restaurant in the same film, there is the Sampson mansion in *Harper*, the Wades's Malibu beachfront residence in *The Long Goodbye* and the Albacore club, the exclusive club in *Chinatown* patronized by Noah Cross and his wealthy associates. These places represent a world of plenitude and privilege which is a long way from the empty spaces of urban poverty in classic noir – even though lavishly appointed interiors do feature in classic private eye movies, such as the homes of Lydecker or Laura in *Laura* or the Sternwoods' mansion in *The Big Sleep*.

The gambling ship in *Farewell, My Lovely*.

The Wades's beachfront home in *The Long Goodbye*.

However, the places which the rich inhabit or frequent in this later tradition also function as 'lounge spaces'. They are occupied by lonely, disaffected people whose wealth has removed the necessity of working for a living and seems also to have removed any pleasure or purpose to their lives. Elaine Sampson and Eileen Wade, for example, seem to do little other than sit around, passing the time, brooding about what went wrong in their relationships, flirting with other men. Although they are each part of a family, their roles as wife or mother have dissolved into meaninglessness. It is clear that Mrs Sampson's relationship with her daughter Miranda has broken down, and Eileen Wade is powerless to prevent her husband slowly drinking himself to death.

The locations may look unrecognizable from those a few decades earlier, but 'lounge time' extends into the 1960s and '70s.[31] Considered together, the second wave films present us with a community of people which does not really amount to a community. Instead of belonging to the same 'home', they are just individuals who happen to exist in the same space, going through the motions, with no sense of goal or purpose. This, too, explains the interest in films of the era with the shallow world of the privileged young: the

Miranda by the pool in *Harper*.

kittenish Miranda Sampson dancing by her garden swimming pool as she has nothing else to do; the disco or Mama Reese's bar in *Klute*, full of hip college students and prostitutes; or the hedonist girls on the balcony opposite Marlowe's apartment in *The Long Goodbye*, smoking pot and dancing naked. The air of ethical rectitude which hangs over the original private eye movies (despite the protagonist's inability or unwillingness to impose this on his world) can be detected in the portrayal of these spaces in the films of the 1970s, widely perceived as an era of moral decline.

California Lounging: *The Long Goodbye*

'Your husband keeps some lousy company, Mrs Sampson. As bad as there is in LA. And that's as bad as there is.' – *Harper*

What almost all of the places belonging to the wealthy and the decadent have in common, besides their 'lounge' function, is that they are located in California, a practically ubiquitous presence in the second wave of noir private eye movies. While far from exclusive (*Klute* begins in Pennsylvania and moves to New York; important sections of *Night Moves* take place in Florida; and the sequel to *Harper*, *The Drowning Pool*, 1975, sees Harper despatched to

Bayou country in Louisiana), considered as a group, it is striking how sustained the Californian perspective is.

California is often the setting for early private-eye films, such as *The Maltese Falcon* or *The Big Sleep*, and remains the location for even the most radical later reappropriations of its conventions, such as *Blade Runner*, set in a futuristic LA in 2019, and the 'high school' noir *Brick*. But the movies of the second wave indicate that the list of recurrent 'lounge spaces' requries its own Californian sub-section. There are California's 'shabby rooming houses and hotel lobbies, its private clubs set back on long driveways in the hills, its gambling ships, its dry-out spas in the desert, its manzanita trees, its dingy office interiors, the juxtaposition of its clearly demarcated dreary and luxurious zones'.[32]

The ubiquity of California should come as no real surprise, given that the state is Chandler's and Marlowe's home – and most of these movies are, broadly speaking, Chandleresque in their ambivalent fascination with the dysfunctionality of the rich and the picaresque nature of their private eyes. More starkly than in classic noir, these films display a distinctive feature of 'prose romance', according to Northrop Frye's classic definition of the genre:[33] the fascination not simply with coteries of people living in an idealized, hermetically sealed 'microworld', but especially those who are

Ridley Scott's LA of the future in *Blade Runner*.

privileged and wealthy. Where in some prose fiction traditions this means aristocracy or inherited wealth, here the focus is on the rich communities in California which had originally provided hope for those in other parts of the u.s. after the Second World War with the promise of new jobs in the automobile or aviation industries and brand new housing, before becoming, in the 1960s and '70s, little more than privileged playgrounds for the wealthy. This pushed the poor further into the city of la itself, into housing 'projects', such as Watts and Compton, which themselves were intended to provide the opportunity for a new start.

One obvious difference between the first and second waves of the private eye movie is that films of the later period could exploit bigger budgets and advances in filming techniques, and shoot on location rather than in the studio. These facts alone go some way to explaining the use of more expansive locations and actual exteriors in the later films. It does not quite account for the preoccupation with California, however. If one were seeking to update the noir template by shooting outdoors, surely one would choose the oppressive parts of industrial supercities like New York and Chicago rather than a state famous for its sunshine, beauty and open spaces? Yet despite the bright sunlight and the expansive desert or mountain settings we find in films like *Harper* or *Chinatown*, the Californian world is nevertheless revealed as noir in more subtle and complex ways – especially if we bear in mind Borde's and Chaumeton's looser definition of noir as that which is 'black' for the moviegoers of a particular era.

California, the Golden State, more than any other in the u.s., symbolized the hope and economic comfort of the country – a heady combination of standard u.s. frontier mythology (California is the Western-most state, and the location for the discovery of gold in 1848) and the ideology of economic betterment through enterprise and entrepreneurship. This association with positivity and prosperity is itself a trigger for dissatisfaction, as it stands to reason that corruption in a potential utopia is felt especially bitterly. It was also clear to many, not least to the original writers of hard-boiled fiction – all based in the state[34] – that California was missing something. What was absent was, in William Marling's rather odd phrase, 'conflict and technology'.[35] California lacked an industrial base and this had the effect of intensifying the curious lack of purpose and society in its disparate communities.

California, in other words, figures as one gigantic 'lounge space' in private eye movies in the 1960s and '70s, a way of representing the lost sense of belonging which affects a whole community. Just as the air of 'homelessness' and dislocation in classic noir movies expressed the unease which beset the U.S. in the aftermath of the Second World War, so the use of California in the movies two or three decades later reflects the appetite for unflinching self-analysis of the time. American was digging down into matters close to home, and found itself disgusted by what it uncovered. One thing this introspection exposed was the truth about how fragmented life in modern America had become. Fredric Jameson has said that, in Chandler's fiction, California figures as a 'microcosm and forecast' of America as a whole – not so much as a representation of what it *was* at the time he wrote his novels (in the 1940s and '50s), but as a prediction. The suggestion is that the kind of dislocated, atomized reality of life in one U.S. state, in which individuals and indeed different classes of people were separated from each other, would soon apply to the U.S. as a whole.[36] By the time of the second wave of detective movies, this was no longer prediction but diagnosis.

But the anxiety about America-as-home is also an expression of the disillusionment and shame brought on by traumatic political events such as Watergate and Vietnam. The dominant theme of

Harper and *Chinatown* is that the crimes which the private eye investigates turn out to be perpetrated by politicians or wealthy people with considerable political influence. The ones who are supposed to be running home affairs, looking after the State 'housekeeping', are exposed as untrustworthy and malicious. *Chinatown* depicts LA as governed by a crooked band of power-brokers doing their best to cover their tracks. The psychopathic criminal Augustine in *The Long Goodbye* boasts that his three-acre home is 'across the street from President Nixon' – an association which, in a film released in the middle of the Watergate scandal, is telling.

The message is delivered most powerfully in private eye films by an emphasis on the collapse, cancellation or dissatisfactions of the private eye's domestic life. In *Night Moves*, Harry Moseby's immersion in investigative work has inevitably led his domestic life to suffer, and his wife is openly having an affair with another man. The devastating results are clear in a scene when Harry returns from work and has to break into his own home, to find his wife spending a romantic evening with his cuckolder. His home has become unhomely to him, an alien space, as a result of his work.

More powerful still is *The Long Goodbye*, a film which presents us with an oddly domesticated Marlowe. We first see him at home – not working – having run out of food for his cat, his only loyal companion. As he goes to the all-night store to get some cat food, he offers to bring back milk for the girls in a nearby apartment, who call over to him, 'You're the nicest neighbour we've ever had!' Marlowe replies, 'Gotta be the nicest neighbour. I'm a private eye.' The idea of the private eye as the good neighbour scales down a familiar grand theme – that of the private detective as the only figure in a fragmented, lawless world able to bring about justice and restore the health of society – into something more modest

The domestic detective: *The Long Goodbye*.

and domestic. The implication is that because he is so ill-equipped to solve the bigger problems (for example, the problems of local government which are central to *Harper* and *Chinatown*) he is better off dealing with those in his own locale.

But he is unable even to do this task. Elliott Gould's shabby, shambling take on Marlowe portrays him as probably the least effective of the private eyes in this era (though Harry Moseby comes close). The case he is working on revolves around the mystery of whether or not Marlowe's friend Terry Lennox killed his wife. Woven into this story is a secondary intrigue about the whereabouts of the novelist Roger Wade. But Marlowe cannot

'Gotta be the nicest neighbour': *The Long Goodbye*.

The shocking end of *The Long Goodbye*.

bring Augustine to any kind of justice: Wade drowns himself only yards away from him and, most glaring of all, the detective is unable to guess until the end that Lennox was indeed guilty of arranging for his wife to be killed so he could move to Mexico to begin a new life with his lover.

The shocking end to the film sees Marlowe finally snap when catching up with Lennox in Mexico and – in an act which constitutes a radical departure from the original novel and the nature of its famous protagonist – shooting him dead in cold blood, before spitting on the ground. 'Nobody cares but me', he says. To corroborate Terry's taunt that he is a 'loser', he points out that 'I even lost my cat'. The film ends with him out in the open, apparently exiled on a dusty road in Mexico, walking home, no doubt, but to what kind of home is unclear.

'What a World': The Private Eye's Connective Function

So ineffectual does Altman's Marlowe appear that it is not surprising that he seems to have no office at all, not even an apartment that doubles as workplace (as is the case in *Harper*). He goes through the motions of work simply because he does not know what else to do. Nevertheless, it is this emphasis on work which provides the crumb of comfort in this and other 1970s private eye movies.

Comfort is hard to find in the detective movies of this era. The three best and most representative films end on a similar note of despair. Marlowe's 'Nobody cares but me' echoes Harper's 'Who cares?', while Jake Gittes in *Chinatown* is urged to 'forget it'. The second wave of private eye movies in the 1960s and '70s thus complements the interrogation of space in the original cycle of noir movies by reinforcing the air of domestic crisis and suggesting it is more widespread. The gaze of the private eye comes to seem like that of the disillusioned American Everyman, observing the ruins of a once great country. All he can really do is watch as everything crumbles around him. The impression which *The Long Goodbye*, *Harper*, *Chinatown* and *Night Moves* give is that the detective can only muddle through small, local investigations, such as the missing-persons case (central to the plots of all of these films) while remaining powerless to isolate and extinguish the deeper social and political causes.

Nevertheless, these detectives work just as ferociously as their predecessors. We must not be fooled by their outwardly casual or insouciant demeanour. They labour tirelessly on their cases, visiting one location after another, meeting people and interviewing them, fending off or succumbing to attack. The majority of private eyes of the era (though there are important exceptions, such those in *Night Moves* and especially *Klute*, which will be considered in the next chapter) are versions of the wandering Chandleresque hero. They are even more mobile than the private eyes of the 1940s and '50s – naturally enough, given the increased ground they have to cover and the different locations they have to investigate. Rather than walking from place to place like the *flâneur* – and like Spade in *The Maltese Falcon* – the wandering heroes in these movies travel by car. It is this mobility

The second-wave roaming detective (*Harper*).

and work ethic that point to an implicit restorative dimension of the 1970s detective.

The absence of an office in *The Long Goodbye* is really a red herring. It is true that fewer scenes take place within a traditional private detective's office than in classic noir films. Only *Chinatown* begins conventionally, with the detective being visited in his office by a mysterious client. The first scene in *Harper* ends with the eponymous private eye leaving his dingy studio flat and the camera revealing a plaque on his door: 'Lew Harper, Private Investigations'. The metaphorical logic of classic noir private eye movies is now a reality: there is no pretence about having separate personal and professional realms any more: work has taken over the home.

But what this means is that the private eye's office has actually extended metaphorically outwards in these films. Jameson calls the office in Chandler's fiction almost 'a well-nigh ontological category' because it is a space which 'subsumes a much wider variety of social activity than it is normally understood to do'.[37] He conceives of the office, however, not as purely a *working* space, which is how blue-collar society would conceive of it, but according to the bourgeois conception of it, as a space 'of retreat and withdrawal', where its owner can do what it is that matters to him rather than simply fulfil obligations. This means, Jameson argues, that 'figurative offices' can be found everywhere in Chandler's fiction, such as the 'sumptuous private houses of the various gigolos' in novels such as *Farewell, My Lovely* or *The Lady in the Lake*,[38] or Geiger's pornographic bookstore in *The Big Sleep*.

The office does not function in quite this way in private eye cinema. Film noirs lack Chandler's essentially bourgeois worldview. Nor do adaptations of his fiction seek to emulate the lengthy prose descriptions of its locations. The office in private eye films is decidedly a workspace, with even the most well-appointed examples, such as Jake Gittes's, being used to advance business: it is a place where the detective can receive clients, take phone calls, and pick up packages he has sent to himself in the mail. Yet Jameson's idea of the office as ontological category, a layer of existence in itself, is a suggestive one in the context of the private eye's compulsion to work. Every space he goes into becomes animated by his work's objectives, and therefore, figuratively, he transforms the spaces he enters in the course of his investigation – the hotel rooms, apartments, nightclubs, beachside houses, religious mountain retreats, gambling ships, retirement homes, and so on – at least temporarily, into 'offices'.

There is another echo here of the nineteenth-century *flâneur*, who turned the exterior city street into his 'interior', making himself as much at home in that street as he would be in his study.[39] It would be stretching things too far to suggest that the private eye achieves a *flâneur*-like mastery over the chaotic elements of urban life as a result, but the private eye's access to all areas provides a salve to the bleak picture of 1970s California/America as hopelessly atomized and fragmented.

In his reading of Chandler, Jameson argues that part of what he sees as the quintessential modern American experience of being separated from others, of being unable to merge the various solitudes of mid-twentieth-century existence into some kind of collective experience, is a 'need to be linked by some external force'.[40] This, he suggests, is precisely the function of the detective, who moves through the dislocated Californian spaces as if on an 'episodic', 'picaresque' quest. In Marlowe, Jameson says, Chandler found a figure 'who can be superimposed on the society as a whole, whose routine and life pattern serve somehow to tie its separate and isolated parts together' and who can provide a replacement for the absence of 'any experience in which the whole of the social structure can be grasped'.[41]

Jameson's reading of the literary Marlowe fits with the character's depictions in cinema in the 1970s. Even the ineffectual Marlowe in *The Long Goodbye* is the only person who can enter both of the disparate, typically Californian, communities of the film: the neighbourhood in downtown LA, home to Marlowe himself, and the gated community in Malibu where the affluent yet desperately unhappy couple, Roger and Eileen Wade, live in a splendid apartment on the beach. There is little meaningful contact among the members of either community, and each is entirely separate from the other. Marlowe, however, symbolically 'unites' them. Even the gang of criminals led by Augustine, who wander menacingly into houses in a way that echoes the Manson Family's perversion of the counter-culture ideals of neighbourliness in LA in the late 1960s, seems strangely barred from accessing the Wades's dwelling.

More effective is Robert Mitchum's world-weary Marlowe in Richards's *Farewell, My Lovely*. The twist in the plot is that Helen Grayle, the wife of Judge Baxter Wilson Grayle, who hired the detective to find an expensive necklace of hers, turns out also to be Velma Valento, the nightclub singer whom he was originally tasked to find by the gangster Moose Malloy. Helen has therefore inhabited both kinds of location – the seedy underworld and the cool, self-contained world of the rich – without anyone knowing, because each domain is invisible to the other, and no obvious connection can be envisaged between the two. It is only when Marlowe retraces her movements that the connection is made. Near the end of the movie, Marlowe utters the line originally spoken by Anne Riordan in the novel: 'What a world.' It is an apt remark because, as well as referring to the depth of crime and corruption festering beneath public life in LA, it also links into a single world the disparate locations of the story.

Marlowe gains little comfort from his connective ability, and neither world stands to gain anything of value from his revelations. But no matter. Jameson's point is that it is the reader who 'benefits' from the private eye's connection of separate locations, as it provides him or her with some kind of historically valid overview of the entire world represented in the novel, a useful 'cognitive map'.[42] Likewise in film: because he is able to access all areas and see what is hidden for almost everyone else, the private eye enables the viewer to imagine a virtual community made up of the amalgamated spaces he or she has been watching in the cinematic world. In bleak 1970s detective cinema, this is as close to redemption as he can hope to come.

'My Friend, My Porch, My House': Devil in a Blue Dress

It was not until the more politically optimistic 1990s – though this was a decade beset by extreme polarization of the rich and poor in the U.S., especially along racial lines – that a private eye movie featured the detective performing the connective role without remaining himself exiled from any kind of meaningful home. Carl Franklin's 1995 movie *Devil in a Blue Dress*, adapted from Walter Mosley's 1990 novel, is a late second wave retro-noir, set in 1948 Los Angeles. It is more revisionist than the

The exception to the rule: John Shaft's cultured, luxury apartment (*Shaft*).

1970s movies in that it addresses directly an issue which can only be implicit in classic noir, that of race. Because of this change from the norm, *Devil in a Blue Dress* defamiliarizes and ultimately provides a far more redemptive treatment of the dialectic between work and home in the private eye film than movies like *Harper* and *The Long Goodbye*.

The original noir films were produced at a time when segregation operated in the u.s. and black people were moving in large numbers to the suburbs in la from segregated southern states like Texas, Louisiana and Arkansas with the hope of leading better lives – yet the films scarcely addressed these issues. Black people – ironically, given the label attached to the films – seldom play major roles in noir.[43] *Devil in a Blue Dress* deals with the problem of a movie tradition that ignores black people by making its private eye, who otherwise conforms to the standard Chandleresque prototype of the cinematic private eye (questing, wisecracking, womanizing, at odds with the police, and so on), a black man. Easy Rawlins's picaresque journey takes him into places which were effectively 'no-go' areas for people of the other race: the predominantly black areas of impoverished inner-city (South Central) LA and the residential Watts neighbourhood on the one hand, and the affluent, white, Malibu beach area, on the other. As in *Farewell, My Lovely* (whose missing-girl plot the film echoes) the private eye makes these worlds visible to each other.

An ex-Second World War soldier, down on his luck, out of work (recently made redundant from his job as a machinist in the air industry, a detail which reveals the hollowness of the promises made to African-Americans in the 'Second Great Migration'), Rawlins nevertheless already has his own house, a rare achievement for a black man in his situation. It is something he values greatly. True to form, however, the rhythm of his journeying between the two worlds of the movie – (black) underclass and (white) privileged and powerful – is punctuated by a sequence of violent intrusions into his home: by a pair of corrupt LAPD detectives; by the shady white gangster Albright and associates (whom he finds listening to his music, fixing food from his kitchen and going through his photos) and by another South Central gangster, the black Frank Green, who lies in wait for him there.

But in an upbeat ending which confounds the standard pattern of the second wave movies, Rawlins's home – and work – is ultimately secure. Having cracked the case, he decides to start up his own private eye business, thereby managing to 'become his own boss'. But this private eye is not in it just for himself. While his home has proved vulnerable throughout, there have been hints that the community in which it is placed is more cohesive than those depicted in other private eye films.

He has been prepared for the most dangerous of the attacks, by the desperate Green, through a warning from his neighbour

With my friend, on my porch' (*Devil in a Blue Dress*).

– a black man who constantly offers to cut back Rawlins's trees for a fee. Although the requests are always rebutted, this nameless woodcutter symbolizes a priceless concern for the inhabitants and properties in the neighbourhood. The film ends with the camera pulling slowly back to reveal a picture of a fully functioning community, children playing together, men talking outside their houses, as Rawlins's voice-over concludes: 'I forgot all about Daphne Monet, DeWitt Albright, Carter and them. And I sat with my friend, on my porch, at my house, and we laughed a long time.'

It is a rare moment of community in the private eye movie, an exception that proves the rule. Here we have an affirmation of neighbourliness which is not – as it is in *The Long Goodbye* – undercut by the lack of any real connection between people, and provides a radical contrast to the fragmented, disconnected Californian dwelling spaces depicted in earlier second-wave movies like *Harper* or *Chinatown*. But because it happens to be a black community, it also makes a pointed comment on the genre itself, which is almost exclusively white. As a black man, Rawlins is representative of another category of people who were often literally barred from some forms of domestic comfort and kept, metaphorically at least, 'homeless' in the era of classic noir. His status as detective enables him to improve on the freedoms available to white private eyes in the noir tradition and find a way of keeping the two key spaces of the private detective, home and work, satisfyingly separate.

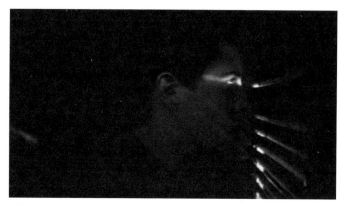

Jeffrey hiding in Dorothy's closet in *Blue Velvet*.

4

Policing: *Gender and Desire 'in the Private Eye'*

'For years now, I've been a man with no private existence. I've had no ideas, no views, no feelings that were absolutely mine. I came alive only in a public situation . . . And then one day, this job was offered to me. I became a detective, a "public eye".'
– *Follow Me* (1972)

Unlike other noir characters – the cornered protagonist, the femme fatale, the countless nondescript patrons of the bars, hotels and diners which make up the 'lounge' spaces of the noir world – the private eye works relentlessly, without respite. One effect of this, as I have been suggesting, is that it both reinforces and complicates the idea that film noir is an anxious lament for the absent home in American culture. The private eye's symbolic 'homelessness' and his figurative linking of disconnected communities compels viewers to consider the value of home, and how this is threatened by the fragmentation of modern existence. But this is not the only result of the private eye's labour.

This last chapter explores three other effects of his detective work: its consequences for other people, especially those whose private space is breached; its consequences for the private eye himself – the man who forfeits his own private life in order to explore those of others; and, finally, how it compromises his efforts

Lounging at home: Hammer in *Kiss Me Deadly*.

to remain truly 'private', or at least free from the demands of a more publicly accountable kind of police work. If the conclusions in chapter Three were cautiously optimistic, here they are cautionary. Rather than considering the question of 'home' in private eye films, this is more a matter of examining some 'home truths' about the detective, about his apparent independence, even his status as a force for Good.

'Doing the Dirty Job': Police Work by Proxy

Why does the private eye work so relentlessly? More than in other films, this question drives the 1966 second wave movie *Harper*. Despite its complex plot, what Harper's work is, and why he does it, is the real unsolved mystery in the film. The flighty and flirtatious Miranda Sampson is especially intrigued by the question. Having noted early on that he 'works hard' (especially in contrast to her own hedonistic lifestyle) she asks him, 'What do you do this kind of crummy work for anyway?' His answer is ironic, evasive and cryptic, all at the same time:

'Doing the dirty job': the dénouement of *Harper*.

> What, are you trying to be funny? I do it because I believe
> in the United Nations, and South East Asia and . . . You
> think it's funny if your life depends on what goes through
> the Panama Canal? What about the English pound? I'll tell
> you something, boy, so long as there's a Siberia, you'll find
> Lew Harper on the job!

So why *does* he do what he does? Clearer – though still rather
oblique – is the climactic exchange between the detective and his
attorney friend Albert Graves, once Harper has realized that Graves
is not just an interested observer but actually the killer he has been
trying to find all along. Graves's moralistic justification for the deed
– that his victim was a repulsive, cruel man – prompts Harper to
recall that, 'when we first met you were gonna push your way all
the way up to be governor of this great and powerful state of
California. That was a pretty nasty and terminal thing you did to
Sampson. Do governor-type people do that today?' Graves retorts
that when they were younger, Harper was going to push *his* way
up 'to being the greatest defender of justice that the great and
powerful state of California ever had', and asks 'How does it feel
to be popping your flash bulbs in dirty little motel rooms, spying
on the cheaters?' Harper replies, 'Boy, I had a total of about eight

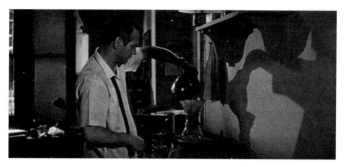
The downbeat detective at home: *Harper*.

disgusting months last year. But then I had five or six good weeks
. . . Those five or six weeks, I really felt alive. So all I can do, Albert,
is just do the dirty job all the way down the line.'

His words articulate the sense of resignation and failure which
is always present in the figure of the cinematic private eye. All his
high ideals and ambitions about justice are reduced to a commitment
to 'the dirty job'. *Harper* confirms that detective-work is not about
glory, glamour, or even financial success. The inauspicious opening
to the film (which prefigures the downbeat opening of *The Long
Goodbye* a few years later), showing him reusing an old coffee filter
in the modest apartment which doubles as his office, has made that
clear from the start. So have the activities he engages in while working. At one point he rifles through a newly dead man's pockets for
clues rather than showing any sympathy for him, and, at another,
while questioning Fay Estabrook over a drink, he admits he is 'feed-
ing booze to an alcoholic to get information'. Doing 'the dirty job'
is justice, only not the kind that is delivered in a court of law. No
justice or even retribution is visited upon Albert Graves at the end.
The dirty job trades in the kind of judgement which involves
exposing corruption to the gaze of others or, as in this case, to the
perpetrators themselves. The payback is thus a small one, but it is
what makes the detective 'feel alive'.

Looking in on 'lounge space': *Out of the Past*.

Part of the payback is the detective's ability to open up to scrutiny the very spaces Vivian Sobchack identifies as typically noir. His investigation involves visiting the seedy parts of town, the bars and shabby apartments that remain largely lawless and invisible to ordinary society, opening such private spaces up to our – the viewers' – gaze. While driven on a personal level, there is undoubtedly a social value to this aspect of his job. More than simply opening lounge spaces up to scrutiny, the private eye can actively *police* them, calling them to account for their disorder. In *The Big Heat*, for example, there is a scene in which the psychopathic mobster Vince Stone punishes a woman in a nightclub by burning her with his cigar. When a patron of the bar tries to stand up to him, he is warned off by Stone's bodyguard. At this point, former police detective turned private detective Dave Bannion, who has been drinking there, intervenes. Warned by Stone's henchman that this is none of his business, Bannion

'Policing lounge' space: *The Big Heat*.

replies, 'All right, suppose you tell me what my business is?', before beating him up and ejecting both undesirables from the club.

Police work is clearly Bannion's business, even though his presence in the club is not part of official police duty (and at this point in the film he is, ironically, no longer part of the police force, having handed in his badge and become an unpaid private eye on a revenge mission). It doesn't prevent the club from being a transitory space peopled with '"loose" women and "idle" men',[1] restless characters (such as Stone's partner, Debby Marsh) who neither work nor enjoy leisure time. Yet it does impose a modicum of order upon it, injecting the dead time-space of the lounge bar with the energy of the detective's business.[2]

Although viewers may thrill to the private eye's bravery in standing up to the bullies, his policing function provides a further corrective to the romanticized view of the detective as hero outside the law, a kind of updated version of the cowboy hero of the

Western. A conservative reading of the private eye film would argue that the function of the detective is ultimately to maintain social order, and provide its viewers with the reassurance which detective fiction has always been geared up to give. Crime fiction has been considered as a validation of the 'panoptic' logic of modern society, reinforcing the ideology that society can – and ought to – be made entirely transparent and scrutible.[3]

The philosopher Michel Foucault's ideas about crime and punishment are relevant here. According to Foucault's theory, discipline is a kind of power that has dominated Western liberal society since the late eighteenth century, and which chiefly involves 'an ideal of unseen but all-seeing surveillance' and 'a regime of the norm'.[4] This is sustained through the kinds of language and activities deployed by powerful institutions such as psychiatry, medicine and the law which promote ideals about what is 'normal' in order to isolate, punish and exclude those who do not measure up.

Central to this process – and something which 'The Panopticon', the circular prison designed by Jeremy Bentham in 1787, does with brutal efficiency – is to fix individuals in 'an enclosed, segmented space, observed at every point' so they can be supervised and their actions observed, recorded, measured and assessed.[5] This works most effectively through places of confinement such as the asylum, the prison, the approved school and the hospital. However, a consequence of the rise of discipline in the nineteenth century is a complementary 'policing' of the private and domestic sphere.

But policing the private brings with it a problem. How do the authorities ensure that the panoptic 'gaze', or at least some form of panoptic scrutiny, can reach continually into private space as effectively as it can into places where people are incarcerated or easily observed and measured? In a democracy, the State cannot directly intrude into the private domain the way it can in a totalitarian regime. Overcoming this problem is central to the work of the police. Police work requires the panoptic gaze to be dispersed among the entire social body, transforming it into one large 'field of perception: thousands of eyes posted everywhere, mobile attentions ever on the alert, a long, hierarchized network'.[6]

In Paris in the eighteenth century – the example given by Foucault – this hierarchy involved a network of *commissaires*, *inspecteurs*, secret agents, informers and prostitutes. Their work created what Foucault calls the 'immense police text' which covered society, in the form of registering 'forms of behaviour, attitudes, possibilities, suspicions – a permanent account of individuals' behaviour'.[7]

Following his emergence in the nineteenth century, it stands to reason that the private detective would play a part in writing this immense police text. This is certainly how the profession functioned in its earliest days when, for example, the Pinkerton National Detective Agency was formed (in 1845) and effectively supported the work of the police while remaining separate from it. The private eye is unofficial and usually at odds with the police, yet his work helps ensure that surveillance can become woven into the wider social fabric. The private eye endorses the panoptic logic of modern society – though not in the manner of the Sherlock Holmes type of detective, the 'unseen seer, who stands at the centre of the social panopticon and employs his "science" to make all things visible on behalf of the forces of order'.[8] The private eye – and this again compromises any view of him as 'hero' – is more like a lowly member of the network of informers, slightly more reputable than a prostitute or an informer, but a long way below the policeman.

'In the Private Eye'

One of the distinctive features of the private eye narrative is the emphasis it places on individual authority. This is conveyed primarily in prose fiction by use of the first-person voice, favoured by writers of hard-boiled detective fiction. It signals that the narrator has authority over the world he enters, despite the danger it poses and the fact that he does not fully understand it throughout. It is characterized generally by snappy, earthy, hard-boiled language, the way people talk on the (mean) streets, and especially by the wisecrack, a tactic which advertises the detective's independence from hierarchies and the experience he can draw on to ensure no-one can fool him.[9]

The literary critic Peter Messent has argued that the hard-boiled novel's confinement to a particular, limited, perspective sustains the impression of the private eye's '*clear-sightedness*'. He suggests that detective fiction constantly dramatizes the 'process of seeing' through narrative sequences which show 'the authoritative seeing eye of the detective at work'. As a result it hammers home a message about 'the authority that comes from close, continual, and apparently detached observation'.[10]

The way that the detective's individualist authority is reinforced at a technical level in fiction is naturally replicated and in fact intensified by cinema, because the medium works by depicting what is seen in the eye of the camera. Cinema specializes in presenting what is seen by 'the private eye' – that is, by the eye of an individual who either sees what no one else is privy to, or who sees things in a particular, partial way. It might be considered (and has been) a naturally 'voyeuristic' medium in this respect.[11] In private detective movies, however, the technique becomes both formal device and part of the particular work performed by the private detective. As I noted in chapter Two, private eye movies are packed full of sequences which detail the detective's practices: scoping out buildings, placing people under surveillance, watching them through binoculars or photographing them, following them and watching them unobserved behind bushes or from balconies.

Some private eye movies have tried to incorporate or emulate the first-person narrative voice in the *mise en scène* and thus recreate more closely the effect of hard-boiled fiction. Examples here are the first-person camera perspective in Robert Montgomery's decidedly odd *The Lady in the Lake*, or the controversial voice-over in the original version of *Blade Runner*.[12] Yet the standard 'realist' cinematic technique, which tells a coherent story from one central viewpoint, and deploys devices such as 'point-of-view' or 'over-the-shoulder' shots at strategic moments to narrow the field of vision to what a particular character can see, is perfectly able to convey the effect without trying to replicate another medium.

The vast majority of private eye movies filter narrative events almost entirely through the eyes of the detective protagonist. Film naturally lends itself to ensuring viewers identify with the hero, but what is striking about private eye movies is that the private eye is on screen for almost the entire film. This is the case in *The Big Sleep*, for example, where the only exception is a scene towards the

'In the private eye': *Manorama: Six Feet Under.*

'In the private eye': *Brick*.

end between the hoods Harry Jones and Canino. Yet even here
Marlowe is hiding behind the door, overhearing or at least guessing
at everything they have been saying. This means that the film only
shows us its story from his perspective. The result is not only that
visually we are rooted to the private eye's perspective but that
cognitively, we can only know what he knows, when he knows it.

Because cinema, and especially what Bonitzer called the 'labyrinthine' movie thriller, tends to operate according to the logic
of 'partial vision', however, any impression of the private eye's
'clear-sightedness' is severely compromised. This is something we
can understand if we examine in more depth the conjunction
between cinematic perspective and the role of the observer in the
private eye movie.

What recurs over and again are moments when the private eye
views the spaces he enters and the people who inhabit them. It is
at this point that the term 'private eye' becomes more than simply
a description of a profession but designates a particular kind of gaze
which, like the panopticon, exposes the private. Here, to quote
Brian McHale, the private investigator is figuratively reduced 'to
the organ of visual perception, the (private) eye'.[13] The fact the gaze

of the viewer is always filtered through that of a specific viewer *in* the film, the private eye, must always be kept in mind. In noir private eye movies the kind of empty 'lounge' spaces identified by Sobchack and Copjec are not just presented directly to the viewer (though of course the camera has selected what we see), as they are in other examples of film noir, they are shown 'in the private eye'.

What does it mean to appear 'in the private eye'? We are familiar with the idea of being 'in the public eye'. This presumes an awareness of a person's behaviour on a collective scale, judged against universal norms. We conceive of those in the public eye – celebrities and politicians, for example – as being watched, scrutinized by a community of people: the public. The implication is that this community shares values and norms, and judges those whom it watches accordingly. In a sense, the same thing applies to those who are not celebrities or public figures, simply when in public. We are conditioned to act in certain normative ways in those moments of everyday life conducted in public spaces, such as streets, shops, parks, restaurants, pubs or cinemas. Being in the public eye conditions one's behaviour so that it conforms to these public norms and expectations. 'The public eye' is really just a metaphor, but the closest thing to a literal version is the panoptic device of the surveillance camera.

To appear 'in the private eye', by contrast, would mean, rather paradoxically, not being aware of being watched, feeling convinced that one is in private, and acting differently from the way one would in public. It is paradoxical because one is not aware of appearing anywhere, it is a state of 'non-awareness'; this is what distinguishes it from the public eye. Throughout private eye movies we see characters caught in this position 'in the private eye', unaware that they are being scrutinized. In *Chinatown*, as Jake Gittes tails and spies on Hollis Mulwray, his quarry is repeatedly shown caught 'in the

Hollis and Katherine 'in the private eye' in *Chinatown*.

private eye', that is, shown just as the detective sees him, by the naked eye, in the camera lens, or through binoculars.

While the world goes about its normal business unawares, the private eye is investigating the underside of existence. This happens in the numerous scenes in private eye films in which detectives look through windows, hide behind doors, or enter empty apartments and search through them. *Chinatown* also asks us to reflect on the ambivalent morality of this business. The opening to the movie reveals a distraught fisherman, Curly, being given a sequence of photos by Gittes which show Curly's wife in flagrante with her lover in the woods. The short tawdry sequence tells you everything you need to know about the 'day job' of the private detective, a man who is 'just a snoop', in his own words.

Here we witness at close hand the anguish of a man confronted with evidence of his wife's secret life – all the while framed by the slightly prurient gaze of the private eye. But, of course, our gaze, the viewer's 'private eye', doubles that of the detective. Curly's story is not part of the plot of *Chinatown*. Its function is symbolic. It reveals how the private eye's *raison d'être* is to display what is normally kept private. There is inevitably something unsettling about this, even though what is 'in private' in detective films is normally something criminal. At such points, the private eye is close to the voyeur, and in *Chinatown* it is no accident that as Curly rapidly flicks through the pictures, the visual effect resembles a peep show.[14]

There are two principal effects of the device of depicting people and episodes 'in the private eye'. Firstly, it exposes the secret motivations, the nefarious activities, above all the desires, of others. Secondly, it exposes, or at least raises questions about, the desire of the private detective himself. Focusing on the private eye's desire complements the above discussion about the 'policing' effect of his detective-work. Desire, as psychoanalysis teaches us, is never simply one's own personal desire; it is shaped by the desires of other people, and especially by what it calls 'the Other' – in other words, prevailing assumptions, norms, values and prejudices, or the things which sustain the judgement of 'the public eye'.

Crime Scenes and Other Places of Mystery: Desire in the Private Eye

The awareness that a view or a scene is framed through the gaze of another is the kind of self-reflexivity which is produced naturally and suggestively by cinema. The movement of the camera is more obvious to viewers than the more subtle narrative techniques of prose fiction. Careful placing of the point of view in film marks out

Through the train window in *The Narrow Margin*.

what is on screen as significant, defamiliarizing it so that the viewer looks at it especially attentively. When we watch the private eye watching someone who assumes they are acting in private, what once seemed ordinary behaviour is defamiliarized until it becomes pregnant with meaning and desire.

At one point in *Out of the Past*, for example, the private detective Jeff Bailey returns to Leonard Eels's apartment at night and finds him dead. He vaults a wall outside an apartment where a party is going on and searches a darkened next-door apartment, which turns out to be inhabited by Kathie, his former lover and now nemesis. He hides there and watches as she acts out her plan, masquerading as one Meta Carson, trying to find out what happened to Eels. Her demeanour at once seems more sinister and troubling because she thinks she is acting in private.

The gaze of the private eye defamiliarizes ordinary, everyday public spaces and the kinds of ordinary private space in which everyone dwells. When placed in the private eye the mystery of a

'Suddenly she wasn't drunk anymore . . .': Marlowe looking in on Jessie Florian's apartment in *Murder, My Sweet*.

person's private life – his or her secret, intimate, hidden being – is foregrounded. Because the emphasis of the private eye movie is not on cognition, this is not a matter of judging a particular person, though there is (as I shall discuss in due course) an important element of implicit judgement according to social norms. Essentially, it is a more simple – yet also more mysterious – process of exposing this person to scrutiny.

We can see how this works in a scene early in *Murder, My Sweet*, when Marlowe visits Jessie Florian, the alcoholic widow of a deceased nightclub owner, seeking information. Though she drunkenly tells him, 'no peeking!', as she searches through hidden documents, he watches her secretly from behind the door. When he leaves, he looks through the window to see her immediately on the phone to someone, apparently no longer drunk. The point of view, in which our gaze is aligned to Marlowe's, invites us to ask questions of the person under surveillance – the kind of questions we imagine are going through the detective's mind. Why is she doing this? How does this surreptitious behaviour relate to her earlier drunken clumsiness? Was that an act, or has she been so troubled by Marlowe's visit that she is shocked into sobriety and action?

Similar 'mysteries' – more minor than the murder-mysteries or missing-persons stories which drive the typical crime narrative, but continuous and powerful nonetheless – are suggested in the many scenes in private eye films in which we see a detective following someone. Hitchcock's *Vertigo* provides a classic example, in the famous twenty-minute sequence in which Scottie, the dubiously qualified – and dubiously motivated – private investigator, follows the unwitting Madeleine, a character who is unknown to the viewer at this stage, too, and has not yet even uttered a word. He tails her in the car, and stalks her on foot, shrinking back behind doors, peering from behind gravestones, taking notes. To an uninterested observer, one who merely caught a glimpse of her, her behaviour would arouse no suspicion. She would be an ordinary person, visiting art galleries, checking into a hotel, going for a walk in Golden Gate Park. Yet here she is also 'in the private eye' and,

Private eye in pursuit: James Stewart as Scottie in *Vertigo*.

as a result, she becomes instantly foregrounded as a woman with something to hide or who has been subjected to a particular ordeal.

One inevitable effect of placing someone in the private eye is a kind of paranoia: when we focus on a person, especially a stranger, their behaviour can automatically seem suspicious. This paranoid logic lies behind Poe's 'The Man of the Crowd', and an enigmatic remark Walter Benjamin once made about urban life: 'But isn't every square inch of our cities a crime scene? Every passer-by a culprit? Isn't it the task of the photographer – descendent of the augurs and haruspices – to reveal guilt and to point out the guilty in his pictures?'[15]

But another effect of the private eye's gaze is much more optimistic, more human in fact: it stimulates an interest in another person. There is something surprising about this, for the crime genre has little time for 'character' in the traditional (realist) sense of the term (apart from the protagonist) – as a 'rounded' person who we believe might exist independently of his or her existence in the pages of a novel or on screen. Yet viewing a person in the private eye, as in *Vertigo*, demands that we ask questions about them.

Similar effects are created in that staple of the crime genre, the crime scene. Its experiment with confining the entire film to Marlowe's point of view means that *The Lady in the Lake* is the most literal attempt to depict what is 'in the private eye'. Curiously enough, it is a failure, because it is forced to find ways of compensating for this confined perspective, such as having characters parading in turns in front of Marlowe/the camera and saying things like 'Why are you frowning?', to enable the viewers to fill in the gaps. Yet there is one highly effective scene in the movie. This is when Marlowe sneaks into Chris Lavery's house and snoops around, noting the open patio door, the unmade bed, the pile of clothes, until he enters the bathroom and finds gunshot holes in the mirror and the shower, and Lavery's dead body. Accompanied by a soft, ethereal, operatic chorus, it is a genuinely creepy episode, as it feels as if someone is about to jump out any moment.[16]

This scene conveys the sense that something we are not supposed to see is being revealed to us: the mundane details of the scene in Lavery's house, such as the pair of trousers thrown on a chair, make us reflect on the pathos of the end of a life. In being guided around a crime scene, we are witness to something normally only seen by police officers – or private detectives. It is an empty, static, space, a typical 'noirscape', but one which bears the traces of an earlier scene full of violence and drama to which we were not party, and a sequence of events which we can only begin to imagine.

Crime scene photography, as Henry Bond has explained, 'records what would ordinarily have remained private, personal, and often intimate – the victims would surely never have wanted anyone to look at these pictures'. He notes that the taboo that surrounds looking at, discussing and researching real crime scene photos (which his extraordinary book *Lacan at the Scene*, does) comes from 'the recognition (or repudiation of the knowledge) that viewing such objects has a voyeuristic dimension, or perhaps

The crime scene in *Brick*.

the realization of an unconscious wish to look where it is forbidden to look'.[17]

The fictional crime scenes in film noir may be less shocking than real ones because they are inevitably less realistic (they are more stylized and 'clean' and lack the horror of the realization that they contain traces of an actual event), but they nevertheless continue to generate prurience as the viewer is invited to imagine the life – and fate – of another individual.

More precisely, what is exposed by the crime scene 'in the private eye' is desire. Another powerful example can be found in *Brick*, when Brendan finds the body of his girlfriend by a storm drain 'run-off tunnel'. We wonder what could possibly have led to the murder of such a young woman in such an inhospitable place? The image – which keeps recurring in the movie, like a traumatic memory – captures the unsettling stillness after the kind of awful, frenzied, activity which produces real crime scenes. Its very composition suggests traces of actions which have led to the outcome, and behind which lie desires – sometimes obscure, sometimes unattached to a specific individual, sometimes guessable. With the dead body of Emily positioned right of centre, immobile, thrown aside as if merely an insignificant object, we are led to imagine that she has either 'got in the way' of, or 'let down', a desperate individual. Both suspicions are verified as the film progresses.

Scenes like these provide an alternative to Joan Copjec's view that the empty spaces of noir, the vacant office buildings, the abandoned warehouses, the empty corridors, are places 'emptied of desire' because their very emptiness 'indicates less that there is nothing in them than that nothing more can be got out of them. They are no longer interpretable, in the strict sense: that is, they will never yield anything new and cannot, therefore, hide anything.'[18] It is an argument which dovetails with Sobchack's contention about the inertia of film noir, the lack of productive activity, the sense that no one fully *lives* in its world. Yet the crime scenes in noir detective movies suggest otherwise. Although static and empty, they are saturated with the traces of desire. In fact, it is precisely the very emptiness or stillness – the 'just-vacated' quality of Lavery's apartment and the run-off tunnel in *Brick* – which conveys desire. An almost palpable sense of recently expended energy hangs over each scene. These are spaces which conceal – but tantalize the viewer with – the mystery of what happened, who was there, 'whodunnit'.

Crime scenes are merely the most extreme examples of the kind of static 'aftermath' scene we find in private eye movies. In the scene in *Night Moves* when Harry Moseby returns home unexpectedly from work to surprise his wife and her lover, the first thing he does is to sit on his sofa and note the two plates and two empty wine glasses in front of him. The objects, and their arrangement, convey powerfully the desire that led the lovers to eat together before, presumably, retreating to the bedroom to make love. The point of view also suggests the desolate feelings of the bearer of the gaze, Moseby. A scene such as this reminds us again that the energy of the private eye movie does not come from the cerebral ordering of the facts, the interrogations, the ratiocinative process, as is the case in the logic-and-deduction detective story, but from the more impulsive actions of the private eye, in particular his capacity to reveal the spaces and behaviour of other people which evidence private desire.

These just-vacated rooms are close to being the kind of 'uninterpretable' empty spaces of noir pointed to by Copjec. No final interpretation can be arrived at simply by the private eye processing the contents of his gaze. (It would be a simpler task for the 'perfect reasoning machine', Sherlock Holmes.) But this is because the places are full of desire rather than emptied of it. Nor is this resistance to interpretation because we are looking into a lifeless world. Quite the contrary. Viewing these scenes through the frame of the detective's private eye reminds us of the deep mystery of what drives another person's private self and private life.

Women, Private Space and the Detective

Though they are, strictly speaking, uninterpretable, the scenes described above do reveal the desire of the private eye himself. Most obviously, what the detective desires is to *know*. His professional identity is governed by his 'investigative desire', his need to piece together bits and pieces of information by such procedures as visiting crime scenes or suspects' apartments, and tailing people or interviewing them until the case can be cracked. This is a very impersonal kind of desiring, however, which bears out Joan Copjec's take on noir as a depersonalized, desireless universe.

The detective reveals his desire when sifting through clues, but Copjec insists this does not mean the process is governed by any 'historical or personal bias'. In fact, the detective represents a kind of 'universal principle of desire'. In trying to close the gap 'between the evidence and that which the evidence establishes' he mirrors how desire, by definition, focuses on attaining an object which promises satisfaction.[19] In this respect the screen detective is more of a function than an individual. For how else would a man whose identity is almost completely subsumed by his *work* desire? He desires in a general, non-personal way, so that his labour is geared not toward individual satisfaction, but simply to service the mechanics of desire itself.

All this sounds persuasive in theory. But specific examples of private eye cinema, and their process of showing what is in the private eye make it clear that while the detective does represent a

'The Eye' (Ewan McGregor) with camera-gun in *The Eye of the Beholder*.

universal desiring principle, 'historical or personal bias' does indeed provide motivation for him, in either subtle or more complicated ways. While the desire to know and to solve mysteries may be 'universal', the chief mechanism used to arrive at this knowledge, the gaze of the private eye, is flawed and partial.

This is clear in two films, *Mortelle Randonée* (or *Deadly Circuit*) and *The Eye of the Beholder*, both of which adapt Marc Behm's noir novel by the latter name. Each portrays a private eye who abandons his professional duty and follows a female killer with whom he has become infatuated. In the original novel, the private detective remains unnamed, except for his nickname 'The Eye'. No doubt because this conceit would be difficult to sustain in a film, neither example chose to remain faithful to the original text in this respect (though the detective's name in the French version, 'Beauvoir', is aptly 'visual'). Yet the name 'The Eye' is appropriate because this is a detective story in which the private eye and his stock-in-trade technique – placing others 'in the private eye' – collapse into one another. He exists only for this particular dimension of detective-work, renouncing any other aspect of life and even the official dimension of his job.

Much of each film, naturally, consists of moments when the detective observes the killer Joanna/Marie from a distance (via a symbolically appropriate device in the 1999 version: a camera fixed to a gun) or up close, undetected. Both films present us with nothing less than the 'private eye' at its purest, a function which has broken completely free of its moorings and no longer has anything to do with the solution of a crime. Its job is simply to penetrate private spaces, reveal what goes on there – without judgement – in a way which exposes not just the occluded desires of the object of the gaze but the secret desire of its bearer, 'the eye of the beholder'. As the old saying goes, beauty is in the eye of the beholder. Private desire, in other words, transforms what one sees into something different from its perception by another.

Both films show that the main threat to the detached desire of the detective, aligned to 'universal' principles of desire, is the sexual desire for a particular woman. The issue of man as bearer of gaze and woman as object returns us to the charged sexual politics of noir. It is striking how often women happen to be depicted in the private eye, whether they are criminals (as in *Mortelle Randonée* and *The Eye of the Beholder*), innocent victims (Evelyn in *Chinatown*) or suspicious minor characters (Jessie Florian in *Murder, My Sweet*). Desire for women and the troubling nature of woman's desire have been constant themes of film noir criticism since the feminist revolution in film studies in the 1970s, especially in relation to the iconography of the femme fatale.[20] Time and again, noir emphasizes woman's sexual power, through images of her holding cigarettes or guns and through shots of her body, especially her long legs. The threat this power poses to masculinity requires that the film symbolically immobilize or contain the femme fatale by presenting us with counter-images which show her as 'actually or symbolically imprisoned' (for example, 'behind visual bars' in *The Maltese Falcon*, 'happy in the protection of a lover' in *The Big Sleep*, or dead in *Murder, My Sweet*, *Out of the Past* and *Kiss Me Deadly*).[21]

This is not just a noir phenomenon, according to the most famous theory of the cinematic gaze, advanced in Laura Mulvey's essay 'Visual Pleasure and Narrative Cinema' (1975). Mulvey argues that cinema always sets up conditions in which the female figure is imprisoned by the male gaze. Cinematic 'conditions of screening and narrative conventions give the spectator an illusion of looking in on a private world', and this produces voyeuristic pleasure for the male spectator which depends upon viewing the woman as a pleasurable 'object'. Even if the actual viewer of the film is female, the process forces her to adopt a 'masculine' viewpoint on the spectacle.[22]

This mechanism operates, of course, in most private eye films. Many examples contain scenes where the dangerous beauty of a woman is 'trapped' in the gaze of the private detective, as it is repeatedly in *Mortelle Randonée* and *The Eye of the Beholder*. An even greater violation takes place when a detective physically intrudes into the private rooms of a woman in order to subject them to scrutiny.

The desire to penetrate private places and unlock the secrets of those who inhabit them is also a feature of armchair detective fiction. In Conan Doyle's 1891 story 'A Case of Identity', Sherlock Holmes, rather oddly, fantasizes that he and Watson 'could fly out of that window hand in hand, hover over this great city, gently remove the roofs, and peep in at the queer things which are going on'.[23] Holmes's wish remains a fantasy and is, in any case, triggered by a conviction that the 'queer things' would inevitably be criminal. The private eye, however, with his habit of roaming around private spaces, frequently puts such intrusion into practice.

A recurrent scene in private eye movies is the detective intruding into someone's vacated apartment. In many cases this

The brothel in *Farewell, My Lovely*.

means casing over an obviously 'criminal space', either the private residence or the hideout of a suspect or criminal. We might think here of the brothel in *Farewell, My Lovely* run by Frances Amthor (the novel's original 'Psychic Consultant' Jules Amthor imaginatively recast in this second adapation as a large, no-nonsense 'Madame') or more obviously dangerous places such as the apartment of the serial killer in *Seven* (1995) which the two private detectives must enter. Intrusion is full of danger for the detective. This is emphasized in the rare examples of revisionist private eye movies featuring female detectives. In *The Silence of the Lambs* (1991) or *Copycat* (1995), for example, we watch tense episodes where the protagonist pushes her way ever deeper into the dark spaces of a dangerous man's home. Entering criminal spaces is part of the job of the private eye. It adds to the suspense of the film, and fulfils the official 'policing' dimension of the private detective.

But there are many scenes in private eye movies in which the male detective 'colonizes' another's private space when not under immediate threat. It is difficult to watch such scenes without thinking of the figure of the criminal. In Christopher Nolan's short neo-noir, *Following* (1999), the cat burglar Cobb reflects on his job by insisting that stealing things is 'not the point, that's just work'. The point is about 'being here. Entering someone's life, finding out who they are'[24] – and it would seem to apply to some private eyes.

The criminal connotations are especially notable in episodes where a male detective intrudes into a woman's private space. In *Out of the Past*, for example, Bailey walks through a woman's open patio doors at night as she sleeps. His status as detective provides a valid reason for the intrusion and reduces the voyeuristic implications, but the scene supports feminist arguments about how women in film noir are controlled and disempowered.

The detective transfixed: *Laura*.

Fireside Scenes 1: *Laura*

I would like now to consider two especially interesting examples at greater length: Otto Preminger's *Laura* (1944) and Alan J. Pakula's *Klute* (1971). Both films conform to the model taken to the extreme by *Mortelle Randonée* and *The Eye of the Beholder*, in which a detective is unable to resist the temptations of a woman he is supposed to investigate. But beyond emphasizing the threat posed by sexual desire to 'investigative' desire, they also suggest that this is part of a more complex desire for domestic stability. Both examples demonstrate that, for the private eye, the desire for home is the submerged consequence of his irresistible need to work.

In *Laura*, McPherson seems to become seduced and disoriented not simply by the allure of the eponymous character, but by her apartment and what it represents, and it is a struggle for him to contain its threat. The key scene in the movie is where he helps himself to a drink and wanders through Laura's apartment,

McPherson in 'feminine' space: *Laura*.

ostensibly in a search for clues. He begins by going through the motions of looking through her bureau, tossing aside her journal, letters, and papers on the desk without going through them. These are the kind of documents which might be useful in an investigation, but he is more interested in a different kind of personal effect. He goes into her bedroom, which is a highly feminized space, opulent, mirrored, silken – and opens the drawers of her dressing table, lingering over a handkerchief (conventionally an object of seduction, dropped by a woman to be picked up by a man) then sniffing a jar of perfume.

The impression is of a man intruding into another, alien world. It is a world representative of a different class (one of the themes of the film, which pits blue-collar McPherson against the effete novelist Lydecker), or even era, to his own. Most evocatively, though, it is the world of the other gender. This is what is really exposed in the private eye in this movie. Feminine space – and by extension, the 'mysterious' life of a woman – becomes the real object of intrigue, and Lydecker's nefarious activities merely a smokescreen, as it is implied that this feminine domain is troublingly different from the norm.

McPherson continues to inhabit Laura's apartment in a way which seems to exceed the demands of the case. Soon after, we see him settled in an armchair, drinking more whisky, while the huge portrait of Laura which hangs on the living-room wall looks over him. The detective drifts off to sleep, only to be startled as Laura herself dramatically enters her apartment. It is as if the fantasy is so powerful that it has taken on an agency of its own and somehow conjured up the real person. When the alarmed woman threatens to call the police, he tells her 'I am the police', but without conviction – as if he has only just remembered.

Thereafter the film is about McPherson's struggle to reassert his professional composure and regain control over the case, and over the

'In official surroundings': Laura's portrait is echoed in professional space.

effect Laura has had upon him. That the process is complete is signalled in a scene towards the end which functions as the counterpart to the fireside scene. McPherson brings Laura in for questioning to the Homicide Bureau, where the contrast with her opulent rooms could not be more stark: there is a bare wooden table and chairs, and a spotlight is shone into her face. Yet the image of her in closeup, bathed in light, wearing a shawl which resembles the dress in the painting, echoes the earlier phantasmatic image in the portrait. McPherson asks quick-fire questions, demonstrating his control. Yet to her surprise (and ours) he suddenly decides to let her go with no charge. He explains: 'I was 99 per cent certain about you, but I had to get rid of that 1 per cent doubt.' When she asks, 'Wasn't there an easier way to make sure?', his reply is telling: 'I . . . reached a point where I needed official surroundings.'

McPherson's faltering response underlines the importance and difficulty of keeping private and professional space separate.

He here acknowledges that, throughout, his investigation has been blown off course by his fantasy about Laura, which is represented by the portrait. Bringing her out of this fantasy-space, as well as out of the opulent high-society world she belongs to, and into the workaday professional realm where he belongs, has enabled him to reassert his control. But her response to his admission – 'Then it was worth it, Mark' – reveals, by choosing an intimate form of address which is incongruous with the official surroundings, that his 'professional' solution nonetheless has the advantage of partially satisfying his personal desires too.

Laura further confirms that the noir detective movie provides important exceptions to Vivian Sobchack's rules about empty or non-culturally normative space in film noir. Laura's apartment seems a real home (if a little strange) and the attraction it holds for the detective underlines both how completely the private eye submits to the demands of work and also how he secretly yearns

An uncanny fireside scene: *Laura*.

for a fulfilling domestic alternative to his job. The competing desires are summed up in the parodic domestic scene in which McPherson relaxes in the armchair under Laura's portrait. Unlike similar domestic-bliss moments in *The Dark Corner* or *The Lady in the Lake*, here the effect borders on the uncanny (which, for Freud, was the *unheimlich* or 'unhomely').[25] We have a 'couple', one of whom just happens to be absent and assumed by the other to be dead, sitting by the fireplace.

As unique an example as it is, *Laura* nevertheless speaks for the rest of detective noir in showing that the domestic sphere figures as the opposite of the professional sphere, not simply because it represents a different kind of existence but because it threatens to derail an investigation, to negate the very values upon which detective-work is founded. Domestic space haunts professional space in this movie, just as the private eye tradition as a whole is unable completely to expel the desire for the domestic. The detective is unable to keep his home free from the demands of work, but also fails to keep his professional existence free of the need for home.

Fireside Scenes II: *Klute*

Laura confirms, if there were any doubt, that personal bias informs the desire of the detective, however objective he might seek to be, and that this shapes the course of his investigation. McPherson is ultimately able to pull back from his infatuation and make the choice which defines the private eye: to put work before love. But the opposite outcome occurs in *Klute*.

It is the story of Pennsylvania policeman turned puritanical lone-wolf private eye, John Klute, who falls for a sexually alluring woman, the prostitute Bree Daniels. His qualifications for the job are dubious from the outset. He is assigned a missing-persons case because the man who has disappeared is a friend, Tom Gruneman, and he accepts the case though he has never undertaken such work before. Nor does he even know the city, New York, where he has to work. Daniels is initially a suspect, but, as Klute falls in love with her, he realizes that she is not directly involved in the crime, and so channels his energy into protecting her while continuing to search for the real killer.

Klute's investigation and his desire for Daniels involve the same thing: fixing her in the private eye. The standard techniques with which Klute begins his detective-work – watching her, following her as she turns her tricks, tapping her phone, listening to a tape of her conversation with the killer – become transmuted into an unceasing campaign of surveillance geared towards keeping her unharmed by the killer, until the final 'necessary' step is for him to move into her apartment and effectively take over her life. As Christine Gledhill has noted, this amounts to a thorough act of colonization – taking over the private space of a woman who began the film as the very embodiment of an independent woman, one who uses her sexuality to make a living. We are shown

Klute's systematic invasion of her apartment, first tidying it up, then gaining a key, and finally changing its whole style

Feminine space invaded: *Klute*.

and colour scheme, from the sombre, brooding reds and purples of Bree's bachelor existence, to the cooler subdued blues and greys of domestic life.[26]

The way space is used in the film expresses Klute's desire and its satisfaction. His migration from his basement flat to her apartment, in order to watch over her round the clock, parallels the symbolic collapse of his professional duty and personal desire into one another. The 'spatial story' *Klute* tells is, unusually for the private eye film, about the triumph of the domestic space over both work space and 'lounge' space. Having cancelled out domestic and family spaces in its early stages, cutting quickly from a meal between family and friends at which Klute and Gruneman are present to the announcement by the FBI to Gruneman's wife that he is missing, the locations are the typical noir spaces occupied by the lonely – Daniels's apartment, the basement rented by Klute, the hotel rooms, rented apartments, nightclubs and workplaces in which she meets her clients, and the nondescript offices where the FBI discuss the case.

Yet once Klute moves in with Daniels, the domestic sphere is returned to the film. Initially, like *Laura*, this is done parodically:

Klute and Daniels by the fireside in *Klute*.

The killer watches through the skylight: *Klute*.

at one point he returns 'home' to find her sitting by the fireplace, stroking the cat, and remarks, 'Ah, you're up, are you?' Soon it becomes more touchingly authentic, however, as the pair genuinely seem to care for each other. The film ends with Daniels vacating her apartment to move back to Pennsylvania with Klute, presumably to begin something like a more normal domestic existence. Symbolically, the final shot of the movie is of her empty apartment. It signifies flight from a claustrophic, dangerous world. But it also shows us a private space emptied of all content, hollowed out by masculine desire.

Klute's colonization of Daniels's apartment means that she is 'tamed', albeit in a less brutal way than the femme fatale of classic noir, for at least she is permitted the chance of a fulfilled heterosexual relationship with Klute and a life of domestic harmony. This means, Gledhill says, that 'the fatal passion of film noir, relieved of criminality, can be humanised into a love-story'.[27] While Klute's motives are undoubtedly benign, the disturbing potential of his occupation of her life is suggested by the parallel the film sets up between his detective-work and the relentless stalking of the killer on the loose – a man who turns out to be none other than Peter Cable himself: Gruneman's friend and murderer. Just as Klute tails her, watches her and bugs her phone, so Cable stalks her continually, peering throught her skylight at night and terrifying her with menacing telephone calls.

Gledhill's point is that for all its innovative reappropriation of noir conventions, *Klute* exhibits a typically noir conservatism in its portrayal of women: Daniels remains an object of the penetrating male gaze, and she switches between roles which emphasize her sexuality, domestic confinement and victimhood. It is her complex psychology – manipulative, self-destructive – which is really under investigation, her very gender, in fact. Her own professional entry into the private world of men is eclipsed by the fact that she is subject to the penetrating forays into her life of both Klute and Cable. This male scrutiny is intensified and complicated by the fact that there is a third level of 'investigation' into her private space, by her psychotherapist. This doctor is also a woman and her office is therefore, in one sense, a private, feminine place, safe from the designs of the men who pursue Daniels; but it is also where the contents of Daniels's private self are revealed to the viewer: 'What I would really like to do is be faceless and bodyless, and be left alone . . . There's this detective, and I don't know exactly what is happening or what he wants out of me or anything like that, but he took care of me . . .'

Each level of scrutiny represents a way of penetrating into the woman's private space: the analyst through the discourse of psychotherapy, Klute through his erotic *interest* (he was originally given the job, despite his lack of experience, because 'He's interested, and he cares'), and Cable brutally, through voyeurism and violence. What makes the film especially powerful in this respect is its emphasis on how cinema naturally places its characters 'in the private eye'.

Although it ends more happily and conclusively than most private eye films of the 1970s, *Klute* nonetheless transmits a message about how dubious a practice private investigation can be. From the outset it is made clear that it requires no special skill – that is why

Klute is able to do it – and it is presented as far from noble. Klute's investigation leads to the exposure of a murky private world in which private desires are gratified professionally: the world of high-class prostitution. But, as a result, the film suggests a parallel between the work of the prostitute and the job of the private eye. The prostitute – the ultimate 'working girl', just as the private eye is the ultimate 'working man' – is a person whose professional life is all about dealing in private lives and private desires. Like the private detective she enters private space – and this means not simply the locations where she meets her clients, but their fantasy worlds, which they keep hidden from everyone else – and explores private lives.

The logic of this equation is that there is something about private investigation which borders on the illicit and socially unacceptable. It is similarly 'outside the law' – or, to return to the idea of the Foucauldian 'network of informers' which does the police's dirty work for them, occupies a level not much higher up the scale than prostitution. But the parallel also suggests that the exposure of a person's private self can have dangerous consequences, for it may stir into being something dormant yet destructive. When Cable finally confronts Daniels he chastises her for her intrusions into men's private space:

> I'm sure it comes as no surprise to you when I say that there are little corners in everyone which are better off left alone. Little sicknesses, weaknesses which should never be exposed. But that's your stock-in-trade, isn't it, a man's weakness? And I was never really fully aware of mine until you brought them out.

It is this theme of probing deeply into the private lives of its characters which makes *Klute* a classic private eye movie, rather than its playing with the conventions of the noir hero and the

Daniels's space is invaded: *Klute*.

femme fatale. Gledhill argues that the investigative role is dispersed between detective and killer. But in fact each of three key figures in the film, private investigator, prostitute and killer, place others in the private eye – and their intrusions into the private lives of others is duplicated by the cinema viewer.

Though its suspense derives from the mystery about what happened to Gruneman and from the menacing killer at large, the film is really about probing into the hidden 'little corners' of the lives of three people, Daniels, Cable and Klute. As the initial investigation begins, an FBI agent tells Gruneman's wife: 'I'd like you to know that situations of this kind are not unique, Mrs Gruneman. A man will lead a double life, a Jekyll and Hyde existence, and his wife has no idea what's going on.' The irony is that Gruneman is the one person who does not appear to have had a double life. Cable leads one, and so does the private eye himself, a man who uses his investigation as a cover for his desire to win over a woman and to secure a stable domestic future for himself.

Detective or Pervert?: 'Limit-cases' and the Private Life of the Private Eye

Just as those in the public eye are measured against shared codes of behaviour, so those in the private eye can be the subject of private desire or fantasy. Because the gaze of the private eye is borne by a private individual with no allegiances to any authority except himself and his client (or, in other words, to 'work' itself) it is more prone than the trained professional eye of the policeman to being thrown off course by private desire. At worst, the object of the private eye can be trapped in the gaze of the voyeur: an interested, prurient, observer rather than a detached, impassive one.

At the outer edges of the definition of the private eye film, movies featuring amateur private eyes or detectives-by-proxy explore this blurring of boundaries especially clearly. They reveal that placing a person or a scene in the private eye has a double effect. Not only does it reveal another person's desire and private life, it exposes, at some level, the private desire of the bearer of the gaze. In *Rear Window*, for example, the man who assumes the role of

Rear Window: Jeff's 'police-work'.

Rear Window: Thorwald in the frame.

private eye, L. B. Jeffries, watches his neighbours across the yard for ostensibly ethical reasons. He is determined to do his duty as a citizen, and protect others from the suspected killer across the yard. Yet acting for the good of the public also clearly services his private fantasies, for it becomes clear that each of the private lives he observes reveals something about love and marriage (he sees new relationships, interrupted ones, both happy and unhappy lovers),

Who undressed her? Madeleine wakes after being rescued from San Francisco Bay and put to bed (*Vertigo*).

which is precisely the issue which he himself is preoccupied with, as he ponders whether or not to marry his fiancée Lisa.

Vertigo and *Blue Velvet* both show an investigator becoming obsessed with a female suspect, for reasons which have more to do with their own obscure private fantasies than any official investigation. In each film, the investigation leads into truly private corners of the self – but it turns out to be the detective's own murky private world, not that of the mysterious woman. When it becomes plain that Jeffrey Beaumont's 'investigation' in *Blue Velvet* boils down to entering the secret world of Dorothy Vallens, a sultry nightclub singer, his actions immediately seem suspicious. No wonder his girlfriend tells him, 'I don't know if you're a detective or a pervert.' His enigmatic response hardly inspires confidence: 'Well, that's for me to know and you to find out.'

Blue Velvet's most iconic image is Beaumont hiding naked in Dorothy's closet, peering through the slats, half-terrified, half-excited, as she undresses and then receives Frank, her psychotic lover, as a visitor. Beaumont has accessed the innermost space in a private apartment, and from there witnesses its symbolic human counterpart: what is 'hidden away' in Dorothy's private life. What he sees is an absurd sadomasochistic Oedipal drama in which Frank pretends simultaneously to be both needy child and brutal father in order to sustain his sexual arousal, all the while inhaling from an oxygen tank. This memorable and scary scene is perhaps the purest example of being 'in the private eye' in cinema, the absolute opposite of the 'public eye' (when one is aware of being under observation and of the need to behave according to social norms).

Unaware of Beaumont's gaze, Dorothy and Frank express their private pleasures – which also happen to feed Beaumont's own (Oedipal) fantasies. But although he does not know he is being watched, Frank's behaviour, as Slavoj Žižek has noted, appears curiously exaggerated, as if 'staged'.[28] This simply underlines, however, what it means to behave 'in the private eye', rather than just 'in private' – unaware of any observer yet still performing one's private desires as if one were present.

But while neither Beaumont nor Scottie in *Vertigo* are fully aware of how their desires shape and skew their detective-work, the private detective in *Angel Heart*, Harry Angel, is forced to acknowledge this relationship. This is another investigation which seems at first outward-facing but eventually leads inwards, like a Möbius strip, pointing back to the desire of the detective. Each visit to interview someone who might provide information becomes suddenly transformed into a hallucinatory crime scene, as though Angel has returned to the place of the interview only to find the killer has murdered his interviewee before he gets there. But the killer is none other than Angel himself, prone to murderous amnesiac blackouts. The traces of desire revealed by each crime scene point back to his own desire, and his own past.

It is only at the end that the detective is able to read these traces properly – fittingly for this most Oedipal of stories, after a sex scene between Angel and the woman who turns out to be his daughter, aptly named Epiphany. Throughout the film the detective is unable to look at himself in the mirror. But as his client, the mysterious Louis Cyphre (or 'Lucifer', Satan himself), tells him, 'However cleverly you sneak up on the mirror, your reflection always looks you straight in the eye.' Cyphre has assigned this case to the detective precisely to force him to look himself in the eye, to acknowledge his hidden self and forgotten past.

Angel Heart is a rare example of the private eye's gaze being cast on its bearer, illuminating the dark corners of the detective's own private world. In *Klute*, *Vertigo* and *Blue Velvet* the task of illumination is left to the viewer. 'Limit-cases' such as the ones I have been discussing over the last few pages, films which stretch the conventions of the private eye film almost to breaking point, demonstrate what we 'want' from the figure of the detective (a clear moral compass) by showing us what we do *not* want (voyeurism and indulgence in private fantasy). In a kind of film in which the viewer's point of view is aligned so closely with the protagonist's, we share the satisfaction when the gaze of the private eye uncovers a vital clue, or that we are 'guided' safely by him through moments of suspense, such as the inspection of a crime scene. The danger, however, is that we also share in the voyeuristic spectacle enjoyed by a flawed or perverse detective.

The viewer has an ethical responsibility when watching limit-case private eye films: to look for the gaps between the gaze of the detective and the gaze of a more objective other, to remain sensitive to the distinction between being 'in the private eye' and being 'in the public eye'. The reason the closet scene in *Blue Velvet* can be simultaneously comic and frightening is that we see what Beaumont is seeing – but also how he *looks* as he cowers behind the slats. From an external point of view he cannot look like anything other than a voyeur. The situation is more complex still in *Klute*, where Pakula's distinctive *cinéma-vérité* style places the viewer in an uncomfortable position equivalent both to the watchful private

'I know who I am': Angel finally looks in the mirror in *Angel Heart*.

investigator and the deranged killer, poised in the darkness outside her window. The camera restlessly pursues Daniels, probing closer into her private spaces, so we can see how she spends the evening after coming home from work, what she says, and how she behaves during her sessions with clients and her therapist. Compared to Cable or even Klute, neither of whom enjoy the same level of access to her private spaces, this roaming point of view makes the viewer the ultimate 'investigator' in the movie.

It would seem then that the 'investigative gaze' in private eye films is, as Mulvey says of cinema as a whole, inescapably masculine. And this raises questions about how conservative a movie tradition this is. Even if we correctly identify the points when detective-work crosses the line between what is acceptable or not, are we simply being invited to judge other people according to familiar norms and stereotypes?

Private Eye, Public Eye

The irony about the private eye, as revealed in movie after movie, is that his dedication to exploring and exposing the private lives of others means that he forfeits his own private life and exists purely for the job. The private eye is not private at all when it comes to his everyday life.

The implications of this paradox are brought out most directly in a rare kind of detective film, a non-noir, British, private eye story: Carol Reed's little-known 1972 comedy-romance *Follow Me*. The film was released with the title *The Public Eye* in the U.S. (like the Peter Shaffer play upon which it is based)[29] and the reason becomes clear in a key scene in which the detective Christoforou confesses to Belinda, the woman he is supposed to be tailing to find out if she is cheating on her husband, 'For years now, I've been a man with no private existence. I've had no ideas, no views, no feelings that were absolutely mine. I came alive only in a public situation.' Before becoming a detective, he says, he took menial jobs 'to escape being alone with myself'. 'And then one day', he continues, 'this job was offered to me. I became a detective, a "public eye".' Later, in a close-up scene which strikes an incongruously unsettling note in this light-hearted movie, Christoforou expands further on this definition of the private detective, asking Belinda to look at his eye:

> Do you know what this is? One of the Seven Wonders of the World: the completely public eye which looks entirely outward . . . It possesses the most watchful iris, the most attentive cornea, the most perceptive retina in the Northern Hemisphere. And for 10 days it was focused exclusively on you.

The 'completely *public* eye'.

For all its idiosyncrasies, *Follow Me* starkly reveals the private eye as a man with no choice other than to renounce his private life and ensure his existence dissolves into his professional role; he is 'dead' in private, 'alive' only in public.

By calling himself a 'public eye' Christoforou highlights the ambiguities between the private and the public which run throughout private eye movies. Private desire turns out to be dictated by the detective's duty to the public (his professional obligations), while the gaze of the private eye is at times indistinguishable from that of 'the public eye'. The ambiguity is produced by the detective's agency and independence – by the issue with which this book began: the private eye's status as a *private* detective. This status appears to provide him with freedom from the strictures of the law. Yet, as I stated at the start of this chapter, the private eye's work is ultimately part of the panoptic process by which the detective's work assists the writing of Foucault's 'immense police text' and services the aim of making society transparent, bringing what is hidden into the light so that abnormal behaviour and crime can be exposed, corrected, or punished.

Dennis Porter has argued that the hard-boiled novel is founded upon a fundamental paradox: the private eye's detective-work uncovers corruption throughout the social system, yet does so in order to maintain the status quo.[30] It is a contradiction, Peter Messent has suggested, which is crystallized in the key technical feature of the hard-boiled novel, its confinement of the narrative to the single perspective of the private detective – a device which, as I have suggested, finds its perfect complement in cinema's capacity to depict what is 'in the private eye'.

While the emphasis on the detective's seeing eye conveys the fact that what we are presented with is an autonomous private individual working in freedom from the demands of the power-brokers, able to maintain clear vision in the face both of criminal attempts to obscure reality and efforts by social and institutional power to cover things up, in fact his activity ultimately 'serves the interests of the dominant social order, however repressive and unjust that order might be'. The private eye, in Messent's words, 'may appear to see and act from an individualistic and autonomous perspective, but the detective's agency is in fact subordinated to larger forms of social monitoring and control'.[31]

The contradiction between the detective's apparent personal freedom, his very privacy, and his complicity in public forms of discipline and control is what provides the tension at the famous conclusion to *The Maltese Falcon*, when Spade realizes that he cannot let O'Shaughnessy go. He is caught between his own understanding of the case – which he has arrived at through idiosyncratic methods and in blatant opposition to the police – and the unignorable requirements of the law. His explanation for his decision to turn her in, that his instinct will not allow him to let criminals go free any more than a dog could let a rabbit go free, might be interpreted as a coded admission about his inability to ignore the laws of the dominant orders in society.

Because he is marginal and self-deluded in his belief that he is somehow free from larger patterns of social control, Messent calls the private eye a 'Public Eye'.[32] The private eye's activities demonstrate that the two terms are effectively interchangeable. While private eye and public eye would seem to be opposites, both are the same thing in the context of private investigation. The gaze of the private detective appears to be directed outwards, and involves the detective (though not all detectives manage or want to do this, as we have seen) trying to set aside his *own* desire, with the aim (even though he may have different theories about a case than the police) of serving the 'public good'. More precisely, the detective's scrutiny might be termed 'the professional private eye', for it is the need to adhere to professional responsibilities and ethics which prevents, in most cases, the private eye's gaze from becoming too prurient. But this, ironically, is what causes it to overlap with the public eye.

The 'romantic individualist' ethos which hangs over cultural depictions of the private eye is misleading, for the private eye film is inherently conformist and conservative. Private eye movies ultimately convey the message that either (as *The Big Heat* suggests) society should stay as it is, with any threat to its smooth functioning safely expelled, or that (as is clear from *The Long Goodbye*) it would be better off returning to a previous, more stable and cohesive point in history. The private eye gaze assists in the policing of society, by helping to catch criminals and ensuring that justice prevails. But the way it functions – that is, what it chooses to focus on and the effects it has on the detective who is bound to it – means that its unsuspecting object becomes judged according to more subtle forms of 'policing', and is measured against publicly shared norms or laws.

This is even the case in those examples considered above in which the private eye's 'personal' desire gets in the way of his professionalism. In *Vertigo* or *Blue Velvet* the detective's desire is aimed at unlocking the secrets or private spaces of a woman. It may be a personal attraction, but sexual desire for a beautiful, enigmatic woman is a culturally sanctioned norm. Even a fundamentally benign detective like John Klute ends up being simultaneously fascinated by the sexual allure of a woman and determined to 'correct' her and domesticate her. To achieve this end he spies on her, imprisoning her in his gaze – just like the killer outside her apartment.

Christine Gledhill has argued that 'the dominant images' in *Klute*, such as 'the tape recorder, phone-calls from "breathers", bugging – suggest a prying search into areas of private life and its personal secrets, rather than the plottings of criminal organisations'.[33]

The film is thus more interested in what Foucault termed 'discipline' than in punishing the criminal for the crime. Klute actually discovers the killer's identity too late to help Daniels, who has to save herself. But he is successful in helping to convert her private self into an acceptable public one in an essentially panoptic process.

The private eye's gaze is inevitably in alignment with the dominant prejudices and power heirarchies of his age. Even though its emphasis on 'partial vision' means its visual perspectives are quite different from the punitive god's-eye view, it is in this sense that the private eye's gaze is panoptic. The private eye ultimately sees *for* the public eye, either to service the disciplinary process of measurement and social control, or to reflect the values of a prejudicial, misogynistic society.

The irrelevant private eye: Donald Kimball (Willem Defoe) in *American Psycho*.

Conclusion

'Go write a novel or something, and stop playing detective' –
Manorama: Six Feet Under

The private eye is a figure full of paradox: desired and despised, exploring private lives while forfeiting his own, independent of, yet aligned with, the laws and assumptions of the panoptic regime. Another contradiction is that the character has been subject to a process of simultaneous revivification and decline throughout his screen history since the days of classic noir. Just as the private eye has been updated and reappropriated by directors at different cinematic moments, so he has also been portrayed as increasingly comic and irrelevant.

When the private eye originally appeared in cinema in the 1940s he was an outsider, treated with scorn by the authorities, and was frequently unable to figure out the complex labyrinthine mysteries which confronted him. Yet still he represented an ideal of tough-guy masculinity and anti-authoritarianism which was in keeping with his age. When he returned in the 1970s, though retaining a certain existentialist 'cool', he was depicted as out of place and impotent in the face of a cynical, uncaring world and corrupt authorities. His ineffectual and anachronistic qualities were nevertheless precisely what made him a poignant, if not quite tragic, reminder of all that was missing in the modern world: he stood for moral and social codes that were out of date and unsuited to the volatile 1970s world. The viewers of films like *The Long Goodbye* and *Chinatown*, in other words, felt the private eye's failures as if they were their own.

By contrast, many of the private eyes in the last three decades of cinema (not just in the U.S. but in other countries, too) are made to seem irrelevant or downright corrupt, even as they echo the figure's incarnations in previous movie eras. Consequently, the films they appear in are less likely to inspire sympathy in the viewer, and more often pity, ridicule or even contempt.

Mad Detectives, Outsiders and Perverts: Private Eyes in the Cinema, 1990 to the Present

What is noticeable about the most recent period of the private eye movie from the 1990s to the present is that there have been no serious attempts to redevelop or update the basic template of a self-employed private investigator working independently of the police. Second wave movies of the 1960s and '70s show their protagonists in essentially the same profession as those in classic noir: running their own affairs, able to do more or less what they want (even if they work as part of a larger private investigator agency, as in *Night Moves*, or they are in the pay of another corporation, as in *Klute*). It is rare to find this after 1990: one example is 8mm (1999) in which a self-employed private detective specializes in state-of-the-art techniques of surveillance, but there are few others.

As I have argued, this independence of the classic private eye equates neither with glamour nor financial stability. But it is a model of work which was considered admirable by many in an increasingly bureaucratic and corporate late twentieth-century culture. 'Being one's own boss' chimes with cherished American ideals of freedom and individuality. Yet there is no sustained modern-day reappropriation of this convention in films after the 1970s. Where we have traditional private investigators we find them most often in films set in a previous era: in *Angel Heart*, for example, or *Devil in a Blue Dress*.

The situation complements the development of the contemporary American crime novel, according to Peter Messent, where the 'police procedural', a sub-genre of crime fiction which focuses on the work of an entire police department working together to solve a crime, has supplanted the private eye novel:

> While the latter relies on a model of rule-bending individualism, the former puts its emphasis precisely on procedure and collective agency. A fantasy of extra-systemic freedom and authenticity gives way to a more problematic vision of individual detectives operating through systemic procedures.[1]

While an emphasis on collaboration and community might be regarded as refreshing after noir's emphasis on inertia and disconnected existence, it is problematic because it makes even more demonstrable the implicit constriction of detective-work by the demands of the dominant social order which I discussed in the last chapter.

The parallel development in cinema has meant that the most dynamic and memorable 'private eye' roles of recent times have been played by figures operating either within the framework of a police department or the FBI rather than an independent private detective agency, or are working closely with such agencies. In David Fincher's *Seven*, for example, the two detectives, Somerset and Mills, work on the case mostly in isolation from their department, but ultimately remain answerable to it. Another pair of private investigators are Daniels and Aule in Martin Scorsese's retro-thriller set in 1954, *Shutter Island* (2010), both of whom are affiliated to the FBI. Jane Campion's *In the Cut* (2003) recalls *Klute*'s portrayal of the consequences of a love affair between a detective and a female witness. Though mysterious and unorthodox, however, the investigator remains a typical jobbing police detective, full of the institutionalized professional and personal habits – especially the misogyny – shared by his colleagues.

The one place where the portrayal of the entirely independent private detective has persisted is not in the professional-investigation film, where the detectives are usually individuals within the larger context of a professional crime-solving team, but in the mini-tradition I have referred to which features ordinary people becoming private investigators by proxy, either for money or because they are simply compelled to, especially after suffering a personal tragedy. *Brick* is one example. Another is *In the Valley of Elah* (2007), which features a military police officer investigating his soldier son's death in Iraq with a female police detective, while in *Zodiac* – another retro-movie, based on the real case of the 'Zodiac killer' who operated in the Bay Area of California in the late 1960s and early '70s – the mantle of the private investigator passes back and forth between three men who become obsessed with the case: a San Francisco police detective, a journalist and a newspaper cartoonist.

A particularly notable recent example of this tradition is the Indian film *Manorama: Six Feet Under*, which tells of a struggling novelist, desperate to show his mocking wife that he can be the kind of dominant, stereotypically masculine provider she desires, who takes on a case offered to him by one of his fans. While many of his forays into detective-work are flawed (he is caught when attempting clandestine photography and is unable to develop the photos in time because the studio is closed), he nevertheless manages to bring to justice a corrupt politician who is involved both in a shady deal to build a canal through his desert town in Rajasthan, and in a sinister paedophile ring.

As a deliberate reworking of *Chinatown*, *Manorama* concerns itself with wide-ranging political corruption and the sins perpetrated by the fathers, as in 1970s second wave private eye films. Ultimately, though, the impression from private eye movies over the past few decades is that the detective only tries to solve crimes which impact mainly on himself, as in *Angel Heart* or *Brick*, or is irrelevant in the wider scheme of things, his activities being of no public value whatever.

The figure of the private eye has been marginalized still further, in other words. Detective-work has become so personal that it has no wider social significance. Nor is there any room for individuality within an investigative team. This is clear in the Hong Kong thriller *Sun Taam* (2007) (released as *Mad Detective* in the UK and U.S.), which focuses on a deeply eccentric detective, Chan Kwai Bun, who is gifted with a psychic ability to see into people's inner personalities. The conceit is an interesting variation on the classic private eye technique of opening up private space. But such extreme individuality cannot be tolerated and Bun has been expelled from the police force as a result, and can only help his young successor on an unofficial basis.

The decline in value of the private eye is especially visible when he features as a minor character in a range of different films, from crime thrillers to comedy. Such cameos are reminders of how firmly the private eye became fixed in movie mythology following the influence of noir. Only a few brushstrokes are required – a fedora or sharp suit, the act of ruminatively lighting a cigarette before stepping into a place to be investigated – to trigger in the mind of the viewer the traditional associations with toughness and independence. No sooner are they evoked in contemporary cinema, however, than they are dispelled.

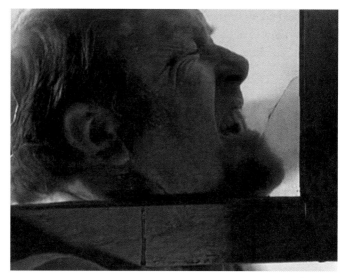

Visser's appropriately gruesome demise in *Blood Simple*.

The apogée of the loathsome, corrupt, private detective is the voyeuristic, double-crossing Loren Visser in the Coen Brothers's 1984 neo-noir, *Blood Simple*. Visser's death is a fitting one for a corrupt, perverse snoop. As he reaches round to force open a window, one of his victims, Abby, traps him by pinning his hand to the sill with a knife. The blow pulls his face into the window, cracking the glass. He is trapped in the act of snooping, his face a rictus of pain – a freeze-frame image of the disreputable private eye.

Another voyeuristic, crooked private investigator features in the comedy *There's Something About Mary*, in which Matt Dillon's insurance claims investigator, Patrick Healy, a clear parody of the Hollywood private eye, is called in to find Mary. But his 'investigation' merely adds to the film's comic probing of the boundary between stalking and masculine expressions of love,[2] as he tails Mary and, upon finding out how attractive she is, bugs her apartment and watches her undress through binoculars. The question which hovers over *Blue Velvet* – is the investigator a detective or a pervert? – is answered here firmly in favour of the latter.

Elsewhere this contemptuous attitude towards the private eye becomes one of mild pity at his irrelevance – a response invited by Donald Kimball, the private investigator in *American Psycho* (2000). Called in to 'sort out all this information' and find a missing man murdered by the yuppie serial killer, Patrick Bateman, Kimball finds – like another ineffectual detective confronted with a serial killer 40 years earlier, Arbogast in *Psycho* (1960) – that he is entirely unable to do so. He can offer little more than a bewildered comment on the peculiarities of existence – a far cry from the wisecracks of the confident noir detective. 'It's just strange', he tells Bateman: 'One day someone's walking around, going to work, alive, and then . . . People just . . . disappear.' After a few visits, Kimball himself disappears from the narrative, leaving Bateman to continue with his crimes, as if to confirm that the private investigator has no place in this world.

Public Interest, Private Eye

One reason for the decline of the cinematic private eye is Messent's idea that a once pervasive cultural fantasy of individual freedom has been replaced by one of collective procedure. Another might be that the conviction of a stable distinction between the private and the public eye is even less tenable than it once was. As I argued in the last chapter, the private eye movie effectively trades on the illusion that the private eye is operating quite independently from the panoptic 'public eye' of the official authorities, offering his own 'clear-sighted' perspective. But the two things end up coinciding and the private eye sees in ways which in fact conform to and perpetuate prevailing ideologies. Now, in the twenty-first century, the distinction between the private eye and the public eye has become even more blurred.

Private investigation has extended outwards, beyond the sphere of either the professional investigator or the voyeur. In private eye movies, private eye viewing is performed either by an essentially well-intentioned professional or by an amateur who has the best interests of others at heart but whose investigation strays into voyeurism, as in *Rear Window* or *Blue Velvet*. But a form of private investigation is today a normal part of life for many people, given the advent of the Internet generally, and social networking in particular. An acceptable kind of voyeurism is sanctioned by Google or Facebook, as we peer into the private lives and spaces of others – places which once, not so long ago, were guarded as private, intimate, secret. In return we show a willingness to exhibit our own private experience for public consumption – through Facebook, Twitter, other online platforms and reality television, all mechanisms set up to enable individuals to *display* their private selves and activities.

To call this turning-inside-out of the established distinction between public and private space 'psychopathological' would be going too far. Yet, in this sense, *American Psycho* (a title which demands to be read as referring to a style or a way of life, like 'American Gothic', rather than merely as a label for its deranged protagonist) is conveying a message which is very much of its time. The point of the film is that Bateman's secret psycho-sexual life parallels his public and professional life. Just as he endlessly consumes commodities (restaurant meals, hi-fi equipment, skincare products and so on), so he symbolically consumes bodies – using them for gratification (via sex or murder).

'American psycho' is a contemporary world in which public collapses into private, and vice versa. There is no distinction between either of Patrick Bateman's lives, professional or private.

It is therefore hardly surprising that a private detective who seems as if he has wandered in from another film, if not another era, should be left disorientated in his efforts to untangle what has been going on 'in private'.

Just as private investigation has extended outwards, so the public eye has narrowed. The ideal of the public, panoptic gaze, which we apprehend 'above us', watching us every time we are in public, measuring our behaviour against normal standards and judging us according to social norms, has come to coincide with a prurient, partial, 'private eye' gaze. Proof of this is the phone-hacking scandal which dominated the UK media during the latter half of 2011. It came to light that journalists at Sunday newspaper the *News of the World* had engaged in a range of illegal activities to gain information for their stories, such as hacking phones and bribing police. Their strategy included using private investigators to do such things as intercepting the private voicemail messages of a range of politicians, celebrities, football players, members of the public, and even a missing schoolgirl, Milly Dowler; acquiring ex-directory phone numbers and addresses of people the paper wished to trace; extracting information from the police; and conducting surveillance and compiling dossiers on three lawyers leading damages claims against the newpaper itself.[3] Private lives were being targeted, penetrated and exposed, caught 'in the private eye' in the name of 'public interest'.

Besides laying bare all sorts of uncomfortable facts about how the media operates and how flimsy the regulations designed to protect the privacy of individuals from media intrusion are, the revelations placed in the spotlight the murky business of real private investigation. Three investigators (Glenn Mulcaire, Steve Whittamore and Jonathan Rees) found themselves, ironically, subject to intense media scrutiny and portrayed as denizens of a vaguely criminal world (two already had criminal convictions).

The case affirmed the kind of contempt for private investigators which we find in movies like *Blood Simple*, and recalled Raymond Chandler's comment that 'the real-life private eye is a sleazy little drudge from the Burns Agency, a strong-arm guy with no more personality than a blackjack' and 'about as much moral stature as a stop and go sign'.[4]

The *News of the World* saga suggests that the private eye is no longer involved in the investigation of crime but in the investigation of private lives – the activity which is in fact now the main function of the tabloid press: to expose the private lives of famous people to public scrutiny. The tabloid newspaper is itself a kind of 'private eye', a way of enabling us to place in the private eye people who are used to being in the public eye. The implication behind such nefarious journalistic activity is that it is criminal to have a truly private life – that is, one which involves anything that runs counter to established social norms. It confirms, too, that no matter how brave or maverick or sensitive an investigator might be, the gaze of the private eye inevitably ends up endorsing the norms, values and prejudices of the prevailing social order and its 'public eye'.

As the examples examined in this book demonstrate, watching private eye films is about more than indulging in male fantasy or deriving satisfaction as our surrogates poke their noses fearlessly into a world of corruption and deceit. They confront us with questions about domestic life and work – questions which complicate the widespread assumption that fictional private investigators are romantic or 'cognitive' heroes. In decline it may now be, but the private eye film has always explored the kind of questions about publicity and privacy which, as the *News of the World* scandal shows, remain especially pertinent to twentieth-first century life.

References

Introduction

1 Raymond Chandler, 'The Simple Art of Murder' (1944), in Frank McShane, ed., *Chandler: Later Novels and Other Writings* (New York, 1995), pp. 977–92.

2 Michael Eaton, *Chinatown* (London, 1997), pp. 16–17.

3 Tim Ryan, 'An Interview with *Brick* Director, Rian Johnson' (20 April 2006), rottentomatoes.com, accessed 23 August 2012.

4 Terrence Rafferty, 'A Gumshoe Adrift, Lost in the '70s [On Altman's *The Long Goodbye*]', *New York Times* (15 April 2007), nytimes.com, accessed 23 August 2012.

5 Frank Krutnik, *In a Lonely Street: Film Noir, Genre, Masculinity* (London, 1991), p. 92.

6 In any case, as Joyce Carol Oates has pointed out, 'private detectives are rarely involved in authentic crime cases and would have no access, in contemporary times, to the findings of forensics experts'. Joyce Carol Oates, 'The Simple Art of Murder', pp. 34–5, cited in Peter Messent, 'Introduction: From Private Eye to Police Procedural – The Logic of Contemporary Crime Fiction', in Messent, ed., *Criminal Proceedings: The Contemporary American Crime Novel* (London and Chicago, IL, 1997), pp. 1–21, p. 12.

7 Steven Marcus, 'Introduction to *The Continental Op*' [1974], in Glenn W. Most and William W. Stowe, eds, *The Poetics of Murder: Detective Fiction and Literary Theory* (San Diego, CA, 1983), pp. 197–209, p. 198.

8 Joseph Conrad, *The Secret Agent* (Oxford, 2004), p. 10.

9 See, for example, Sylvia Harvey, 'Woman's Place: The Absent Family of Film Noir', in E. Ann Kaplan, ed., *Women in Film Noir* (London,

1978), pp. 22–34; Pam Cook, 'Duplicity in *Mildred Pierce*', in E. Ann Kaplan, ed., *Women in Film Noir* (London, 1978), pp. 68–82.

1 History: The Private Eye Film

1 Raymond Chandler, *The Big Sleep* [1939] (London, 1970), p. 23.

2 Arthur Conan Doyle, 'A Scandal in Bohemia', in *The Adventures of Sherlock Holmes* (London, 2004), p. 3.

3 See, for example, Deac Rossell, *Living Pictures: The Origins of the Movies* (Albany, NY, 1998); Tom Gunning, *D. W. Griffith and the Origins of American Narrative Film: The Early Years at Biograph* (Illinois, 1994).

4 The B-movie was an attempt to boost audiences by accompanying the main feature (the A-film) with a lower-budget movie, especially an opposing kind of film, i.e. so that comedy was paired with a thriller, etc. The low budget and the demand for rapid production gave the B-movie a kind of uniformity as familiar filming techniques and conventions were copied. The pragmatics of filming B-movies also played a part in the development of noir styles in that they were typically shot at night.

5 See James Damico, 'Film Noir: A Modest Proposal', *Film Reader 3* (February 1978), pp. 48–57; E. Ann Kaplan, ed., *Women in Film Noir* (London, 1978); Foster Hirsch, *The Dark Side of the Screen: Film Noir* (San Diego, CA, 1981); John Tuska, *Dark Cinema: American Film Noir in Cultural Perspective* (Westport, CT, 1984); J. P. Telotte, *Voices in the Dark: The Narrative Patterns of Film Noir* (Chicago, IL, 1989); Frank Krutnik, *In a Lonely Street: Film Noir, Genre, Masculinity* (London, 1991); James Naremore, *More Than Night: Film Noir in its Contexts* (Berkeley and Los Angeles, CA, and London, 1998); Andrew Spicer, *Film Noir* (Harlow, 2002); Sheri Chinen Biesen, *Blackout: World War II and the Origins of Film Noir* (Baltimore, ML, 2005).

6 Nino Frank, 'Un nouveau genre "policier": L'aventure criminelle', *Écran français*, no. 61 (August 1946); Jean-Pierre Chartier, 'Les Américains aussi font des films noirs', *La Revue de cinéma*, no. 2 (November 1946), pp. 66–70; Raymond Borde and Étienne Chaumeton, *Panorama du film noir américain (1941–1953)* (Paris, 1955).

7 Marc Vernet, 'Film Noir on the Edge of Doom', in Joan Copjec, ed., *Shades of Noir* (London and New York, 1993), pp. 1–32, p. 1.

8 Quoted in Tzvetan Todorov, 'The Typology of Detective Fiction', in *The Poetics of Prose*, trans. Richard Howard (New York, 1977), pp. 42–52.

9 Naremore, *More Than Night*, pp. 40–47.

10 Chartier, 'Les Américains aussi font des films noirs', p. 23.

11 Janey Place, 'Women in Film Noir', in Kaplan, ed., *Women in Film Noir*, p. 35.

12 Sylvia Harvey, 'Woman's Place: The Absent Family of Film Noir', in Kaplan, ed., *Women in Film Noir*, p. 25.

13 Krutnik, *In a Lonely Street*, p. 86.

14 Paul Schrader, 'Notes on Film Noir', in Barry Keith Grant, *Film Genre Reader* iii: *volume 3* (Texas, 2003), pp. 229–42.

15 Nino Frank, 'A New Kind of Police Drama: The Criminal Adventure', in Alain Silver and James Ursini, eds, *Film Noir Reader,* ii (New York, 2004), pp. 15–20, p.16.

16 See, for example, Spicer, *Film Noir*, pp. 227–31.

17 Christine Gledhill, '*Klute* i: A Contemporary Film Noir and Feminist Criticism', in Kaplan, ed., *Women in Film Noir*, p. 14; Foster Hirsch, *Detours and Lost Highways: A Map of Neo-Noir* (New York, 1999), p. 99.

18 While *The Maltese Falcon* has the distinction of being regarded by the majority of critics as the first film noir, it was not the first Hammett story to be filmed. The high-living Nick Charles was based on the detective who featured in the author's last novel, *The Thin Man* (1934), and appeared in six movies stretching from 1934 to 1947 under the banner of 'The Thin Man' (actually a description of the murder victim in the original novel): e.g. *The Thin Man* (1934), *After the Thin Man* (1936), *Another Thin Man* (1939), *Shadow of the Thin Man* (1941). Each film revolved around the crime-solving partnership between Charles and his wife Nora (and part of their success was the genuine chemistry between William Powell and Myrna Loy as Nick and Nora, respectively).

19 The fashion is now to claim *Stranger on the Third Floor* (1940) as the first noir. See, for example, Marc Vernet, 'Film Noir on the Edge of Doom', in Copjec, ed., *Shades of Noir*; and Spicer, *Film Noir*.

20 Dashiell Hammett, *The Maltese Falcon* [1929] (London, 2002), p. 1.

21 These were not the first Chandler adaptations: a version of *Farewell, My Lovely* was produced in 1942, shamelessly retitled *The Falcon Takes Over* to capitalize on the success of Huston's movie, while an adaptation of Chandler's *The High Window* (1942), entitled *Time to Kill*, appeared in the same year. Neither preserved the character of Marlowe, however, replacing him with the detectives 'The Falcon' and Michael Shayne, respectively.

22 Raymond Chandler, 'The Simple Art of Murder' [1944], in Frank McShane, ed., *Chandler: Later Novels and Other Writings* (New York, 1995), pp. 991–2. John Paul Athanasourelis has pointed out, quite rightly, that this oft-quoted passage is actually misleading, for 'Nothing [in the rest of] the essay or, indeed, in other writings, supports the claim that Marlowe is "untarnished" or unafraid': John Paul Athanasourelis, *Raymond Chandler's Philip Marlowe: The Hard-Boiled Detective Transformed* (Jefferson, NC, 2012), p. 16.

23 Naremore, *More Than Night*, p. 152.

24 Todd Erickson, 'Kill Me Again: Movement Becomes Genre', in Alain Silver and James Ursini, eds, *The Film Noir Reader* (New York, 1996), p. 321.

25 Spicer, *Film Noir*, p. 133.

26 Fredric Jameson, *Postmodernism, or the Cultural Logic of Late Capitalism* (London and New York, 1991), p. 11, cited in Spicer, *Film Noir*, p. 134.

27 Spicer, *Film Noir*, p. 135.

28 Gledhill, '*Klute* 1', p. 20.

29 This is a point which seemed entirely lost on Michael Winner who, following the success of Robert Mitchum as Marlowe in Richards's *Farewell, My Lovely*, remade *The Big Sleep* with the actor in the same role, only to transpose its original Californian setting to Britain. The result is that Marlowe comes to seem a lost and bewildered figure, despite his best intentions, out of place in the assured social context of suburban semis, penthouses in West London and peculiarly British locations such as 'Hunt's Garage'.

30 See Bran Nicol, *The Cambridge Introduction to Postmodern Fiction* (Cambridge, 2009).

31 Linda Mizejewski, *Hard Boiled and High Heeled: The Woman*

Detective in Popular Culture (London and New York, 2004).

32 Spicer, *Film Noir*, pp. 150–3.

33 As a way of underlining the fact that my three categories are not to be
    taken as rigididly historical, we should note that *Blade Runner* is not
    the first combination of sci-fi and private eye film. This distinction
    belongs to Jean-Luc Godard's *Alphaville: une étrange aventure de
    Lemmy Caution* (1965), a film about a secret agent/private detective,
    Lemmy Caution, who is despatched on a missing-persons case to the
    space city, Alphaville, which he finds under the grip of a despotic ruler.

34 Only three of the director's early pre-noir British films, *Blackmail*
    (1929), *Number 17* (1932) and *Sabotage* (1946), feature detectives,
    while in his mature phase, for example, in *Shadow of a Doubt* (1943),
    Stage Fright (1950), *Dial M for Murder* (1954) and *Frenzy* (1972),
    detectives appear only as minor characters. *Psycho* (1960) might be
    considered a rearranged noir detective story, as the private detective,
    Milton Arbogast, picks up the trail of the missing Marion Crane. But
    he is swiftly dispensed with in order to deepen the intrigue about the
    killer and the sense of danger. Other Hitchcock movies feature
    characters who are professional investigators, if not detectives, such as
    the journalists in *Foreign Correspondent* (1940) or Cary Grant's
    government spy in *Notorious* (1946).

*2 Seeing: Literature, Film and the World of the
    Private Eye*

1 Edgar Allan Poe, 'The Man of the Crowd', in *The Fall of the House of
   Usher, and Other Stories* (Harmondsworth, 1986), pp.179–88, p. 179.

2 Walter Benjamin, *Charles Baudelaire: A Lyric Poet in the Era of High
   Capitalism*, trans. Harry Zohn (London and New York, 1983), p. 48.

3 Poe, 'The Man of the Crowd', p. 179.

4 Patricia Merivale, 'Gumshoe Gothics: Poe's "The Man of the
   Crowd" and his Followers', in Merivale and Susan Elizabeth
   Sweeney, *Detecting Texts: The Metaphysical Detective Story from Poe to
   Postmodernism* (Philadelphia, PA, 1999), pp. 101–16, p. 109.

5 William Brevda, 'Search for the Originary Sign of Noir: Poe's "Man
   of the Crowd"', *Mythosphere*, II/4 (November 2000), pp. 1–7.

6 Walter Benjamin, 'On Some Motifs in Baudelaire', *Illuminations*,

trans. Harry Zohn (New York, 1969), p. 171.

7   Tom Gunning, 'Urban Spectatorship, Poe, Benjamin, and *Traffic in Souls* (1913)', *Wide Angle*, XIX/4, 1997, pp. 25–61; p. 32.

8   Christine Gledhill, '*Klute* 1: Contemporary Film Noir and Feminist Criticism', in E. Ann Kaplan, ed., *Women in Film Noir* (London, 1978), pp. 6–21; p. 15.

9   Frank Krutnik, *In a Lonely Street: Film Noir, Genre, Masculinity* (London, 1991), p. 93.

10   Paul Auster, *City of Glass*, in *The New York Trilogy* (London, 1987), p. 8.

11   Wladimir Krysinski, *Carrefours de signes: Essais sur le roman moderne* (The Hague, 1981); Douwe Fokkema and Elrud Ibsch, *Modernist Conjectures: A Mainstream of European Literature* (London, 1987).

12   Brian McHale, 'The (Post)Modernism of *The Name of the Rose*', in *Constructing Postmodernism* (London, 1992), p. 147.

13   Raymond Chandler, 'The Simple Art of Murder' [1944], in Frank McShane, ed., *Chandler: Later Novels and Other Writings* (New York, 1995), pp. 977–92; p. 992.

14   Tzvetan Todorov, 'The Typology of Detective Fiction', in *The Poetics of Prose*, trans. Richard Howard (New York, 1977), pp. 42–52; p. 44.

15   Todorov, 'The Typology of Detective Fiction', p. 51.

16   Chandler, 'The Simple Art of Murder', p. 991.

17   From Huston's original screenplay of *The Maltese Falcon*.

18   James V. Werner, *American Flaneur: The Cosmic Physiognomy of Edgar Allan Poe* (London, 2004), p. 110.

19   Kristin Ross, 'Watching the Detectives', in Niall Lucy, ed., *Post-modern Literary Theory: An Anthology* (Oxford, 2000), pp. 197–217; p. 202.

20   Christine Gledhill, '*Klute* 2: Feminism and *Klute*', in Kaplan, ed., *Women in Film Noir*, pp.112–28; p.119.

21   Northrop Frye, *Anatomy of Criticism: Four Essays* [1957] (Princeton, NJ, 1971), p. 162.

22   Martin Rubin, *Thrillers* (Cambridge, 1999), p. 18.

23   Ibid., p. 20.

24   William Marling, *Raymond Chandler* (Woodbridge, CT, 1986), p. 78.

25   Dennis Porter, *The Pursuit of Crime: Art and Ideology in Detective Fiction* (New Haven, CT, 1981), p. 39.

26   Krutnik, *In a Lonely Street*, p. 88.

27 In the film version of *The Big Sleep* the specific romance connotations have been replaced by a more general symbolism of 'age-old battle' (e.g. the coat of arms in the Sternwood's mansion).

28 Slavoj Žižek, *Looking Awry: An Introduction to Jacques Lacan Through Popular Culture* (Cambridge, MA, 1991), p. 60.

29 Thomas Pynchon, *The Crying of Lot 49* (London, 2007), p. 85.

30 Marty Roth, *Foul and Fair Play: Reading Genre in Classic Detective Fiction* (Athens, GA, 1995), p. 91.

31 See Greg Forter, *Murdering Masculinities: Fantasies of Gender and Violence in the American Crime Novel* (London and New York, 2000), pp. 11–45.

32 Žižek, *Looking Awry*, p. 60.

33 Foster Hirsch, *The Dark Side of the Screen: Film Noir* (New York, 2001), p. 169.

34 Fredric Jameson, 'The Synoptic Chandler', in Joan Copjec, ed., *Shades of Noir* (London and New York, 1993), pp. 33–56; p. 33.

35 Slavoj Žižek, *Enjoy Your Symptom! Jacques Lacan in Hollywood and Out*, 2nd edn (London, 2001), pp. 149–64; Joan Copjec, 'The Phenomenal Nonphenomenal: Private Space in *Film Noir*', in Copjec, ed., *Shades of Noir*, pp. 167–97.

36 Raymond Chandler, *The Big Sleep* (Harmondsworth, 1970), p. 220.

37 The film version reduces this passage – thus removing Chandler's lyricism and a layer of meaning available to the viewer – to having Marlowe informed that 'in the long run, nothing can save [Sternwood] except dying', to which he replies, 'Yeah – the big sleep. That'll cure his grief'.

38 Todorov, 'The Typology of Detective Fiction', p. 51.

39 Pascal Bonitzer, 'Partial Vision: Film and the Labyrinth', *Wide Angle*, no. 4 (1981), pp. 56–63; see also Rubin, *Thrillers*, p. 26.

40 André Bazin, 'Theatre and Cinema, parts 1 and 2' [1951], *What is Cinema?* [1967], trans. Hugh Gray (Berkeley and Los Angeles, CA, 2005), pp. 76–124.

41 Rubin, *Thrillers*, p. 29.

3 Working: The Private Eye and the Spaces of Noir

1 Borde and Chaumeton, 'Towards a Definition of *Film Noir*', extract

from *Panorama du Film Noir Américain*, in Alain Silver and James Ursini, eds, *Film Noir Reader* II (New York, 1996), pp. 17–26; p. 19.

2 See, for example, Sylvia Harvey, 'Woman's Place: The Absent Family of Film Noir', in E. Ann Kaplan, ed., *Women in Film Noir* (London, 1978), pp. 22–34.

3 Joan Copjec, 'The Phenomenal Non-Phenomenal: Private Space in *Film Noir*', in Copjec, ed., *Shades of Noir* (London and New York), pp. 167–97; Vivian Sobchack, 'Lounge Time: Postwar Crises and the Chronotope of Film Noir', in Nick Browne, ed., *Refiguring American Film Genres: History and Theory* (Berkeley, CA, 1998), pp. 129–70.

4 Joan Copjec, 'The Phenomenal Non-Phenomenal', p. 189.

5 Sobchack, 'Lounge Time', p. 138.

6 Ibid., p. 157.

7 Ibid., p. 144.

8 Ibid., p. 158.

9 Ibid., p. 159.

10 Commonly known by the name of the man in charge of Hollywood censorship at the time, Will H. Hays, the 'Motion Picture Production Code' imposed principles of moral guidance on the productions of major studios in the period 1930–1968.

11 See Sheri Chinen Biesen, *Blackout: World War II and the Origins of Film Noir* (Baltimore, MD, 2005), p. 3.

12 Gaston Bachelard, *The Poetics of Space* [1958] (Boston, MA, 1994), p. 48.

13 A. M. Sperber and Eric Lax, *Bogart* (London, 1997), p. 154; quoted in John Irwin, *Unless the Threat of Death is Behind Them: Hard-Boiled Fiction and Film Noir* (Baltimore, MD, 2006), p. 224.

14 Irwin, *Unless the Threat*, p. 36.

15 Ibid., p. 77.

16 Ibid., p. 36.

17 Marc Vernet, 'Film Noir on the Edge of Doom', in Copjec, ed., *Shades of Noir* (London and New York, 1991), pp. 1–32; p. 18.

18 Dashiell Hammett, *The Maltese Falcon* [1926] (London, 2000), p. 226.

19 Arthur Conan Doyle, *The Sign of Four* [1890] (London, 1982), p. 8.

20 Ibid.

21 Thomas Schatz, *Hollywood Genres: Formulas, Film-making, and the Studio System* (New York, 1981).

22 Geoff Mayer and Brian McDonnell, *Encyclopaedia of Film Noir* (Westport, CT, 2007), p. 58.

23 Sobchack, 'Lounge Time', p. 158.

24 Paul Schrader, 'Notes on Film Noir', in Barry Keith Grant, ed., *Film Noir Reader* III (Austin, TX, 1986), pp. 229–42; p. 234.

25 Dean MacCannell, 'Democracy's Turn: On Homeless Noir', in Copjec, ed., *Shades of Noir*, pp. 279–98; p. 280.

26 Elisabeth Bronfen, *Home in Hollywood: The Imaginary Geography of Cinema* (New York, 2004), p. 21.

27 Andrew Spicer, *Film Noir* (London, 2002), p. 56.

28 This scene recalls an oddly incongruous moment in *The Killers* (1946), noted by Sobchack, when Lubinsky's wife suddenly appears at the door with a pitcher of lemonade and two glasses while he is being interviewed by the insurance investigator (and surrogate detective) Reardon. For Sobchack, the very ordinariness of this kind of unexpected domestic moment simply underlines the fact that there is no place for a conventional notion of home in film noir. (See Sobchack, 'Lounge Time', p. 137.)

29 Fredric Jameson, 'Postmodernism and Consumer Society', in Hal Foster, ed., *The Anti-Aesthetic: Essays on Post-Modern Culture* (Seattle, WA, 1989), pp. 111–125; p. 117.

30 MacCannell, 'Democracy's Turn', pp. 281–2.

31 This bears out Sobchack's claim that the motifs of lounge time can be traced beyond the classic period of noir both to earlier and later traditions, for example 'backward into the 1930s and forward to the present renaissance and radical reworking of noir' (See Sobchack, 'Lounge Time', p. 166.)

32 Kristin Ross, 'Watching the Detectives', in Niall Lucy, ed., *Postmodern Literary Theory: An Anthology*, pp. 197–217; p. 202.

33 Northrop Frye, *The Secular Scripture: A Study of the Structure of Romance* (Boston, MA, 1957), p. 305.

34 Critics have documented how hard-boiled pioneers such as Horace McCoy, Chandler and James M. Cain were committed to countering the idea upheld by a previous generation of writers and intellectuals that LA was a place of promise, 'a Mediterraneanized idyll of New England life [inserted] into an innocent but inferior "Spanish" culture'. As outsiders – not just temperamentally but as immigrants

to California – these writers could see that 'long-standing American themes of westward movement, progress, and self-improvement' did not actually apply to California (See Mike Davies, *City of Quartz: Excavating the Future in Los Angeles*, London, 2006, p. 20.)

35 William Marling, *The American Roman Noir: Hammett, Cain, and Chandler* (Athens, GA and London, 1995), p. 243.

36 Fredric Jameson, *Archaeologies of the Future: The Desire Called Utopia and Other Science Fictions* (London and New York, 2005), p. 127.

37 Fredric Jameson, 'The Synoptic Chandler', in Copjec, ed., *Shades of Noir*, pp. 33–56; p. 39.

38 Ibid., pp. 41–2.

39 James V. Werner, *American Flaneur: The Cosmic Physiognomy of Edgar Allan Poe* (London, 2004), p. 110.

40 Jameson, cited in Ross, 'Watching the Detectives', p. 131.

41 Ibid., p. 127.

42 I am borrowing here the term for the key recuperative gesture in Jameson's cultural criticism. See Fredric Jameson, 'Cognitive Mapping', in Cary Nelson and Lawrence Grossberg, eds, *Marxism and the Interpretation of Culture* (Chicago, IL, 1987), pp. 347–60.

43 An interesting aspect of Richards's *Farewell, My Lovely* is its resurrection of the theme of racism subtly explored in Chandler's original novel, and missing from Dmytryk's 1944 adaptation. The nightclub where Jessie Florian sings is a 'coloured joint' which was once a 'white joint'. 'You got a dead negro. Nobody gives a shit', Marlowe later pointedly tells Nulty, the police detective. The other 1970s films may portray the detective as an impotent figure harassed by criminals and the authorities, but they persist in focusing on what are emphatically *white* communities. A notable precedent was set by the 1972 blaxploitation movie, *Shaft* (1972), in which the eponymous detective has achieved the kind of economic independence aspired to by the hard-boiled protagonist, in John Irwin's terms, and become 'a self-employed, independent operator' (Irwin, *Unless the Threat*, p. 77). While Shaft's office is as modest as others in the private eye tradition, his own apartment is a total contrast to the run-down dwellings of the black underclass in Harlem in which much of the action of the movie is set: it is well-furnished, book-lined, contemporary in style, exuding taste and affluence – features which service the corrective ideology of

the blaxploitation tradition. As well as reflecting his economic success, this apartment also seems to provide a genuine alternative to his work. When we first see him there he is relaxing with his girlfriend, Ellie Moore, and tells her, 'I got to feeling like a machine. That's no way to feel', before a lengthy, indulgent sex scene. This treatment of the themes of 'work' and 'home' place it at odds with the private eye tradition in many ways, though this is because of *Shaft*'s status as blaxploitation movie, a genre with its own rules and conventions.

4 Policing: Gender and Desire 'in the Private Eye'

1 Vivian Sobchack, 'Lounge Time: Postwar Crises and the Chronotope of Film Noir', in Nick Browne, ed., *Refiguring American Film Genres: History and Theory* (Berkeley, CA, 1998), pp. 129–70; p. 159.

2 Sobchack's argument about noir makes use of Mikhail Bakhtin's notion of the chronotope, the idea that genres use recurring recognizable 'time-spaces', historically specific locations which bring together the meanings of the narrative (Sobchack, 'Lounge Time', p. 152). Film noir, with its settings like the cocktail lounge, the nightclub, anonymous hotels and motels, and roadside cafes, creates a temporal existence which 'concretizes' something peculiar to 'character and culture alike' in the 1940s (Sobchack, 'Lounge Time', p. 153).

3 Dennis Porter, *The Pursuit of Crime: Art and Ideology in Detective Fiction* (New Haven, CT, 1981), pp. 122–5; Moretti, 'Clues', in *Signs Taken for Wonders* (London and New York, 1984), p. 240; D. A. Miller, *The Novel and the Police* (Berkeley and Los Angeles, CA, and London, 1989).

4 Miller, *The Novel and the Police*, p. viii.

5 Michel Foucault, *Discipline and Punish: The Birth of the Prison* (Harmondsworth, 1977), p. 197.

6 Ibid., p. 214.

7 Ibid.

8 Porter, *The Pursuit of Crime*, p. 125.

9 Ibid., pp. 122–5; see also Scott R. Christianson, 'Tough Talk and Wisecracks: Language as Power in American Detective Fiction', *The Journal of Popular Culture*, XXIII/2 (Fall 1989), pp. 151–62.

10 Peter Messent, 'Introduction: From Private Eye to Police Procedural

– The Logic of Contemporary Crime Fiction', in Messent, ed., *Criminal Proceedings: The Contemporary American Crime Novel* (London and Chicago, IL, 1997), pp. 1–21; p. 6.

11 Laura Mulvey, 'Visual Pleasure and Narrative Cinema' [1975], in Lizbeth Goodman, ed., *Routledge Reader in Gender and Performance* (London, 1998), pp. 270–75; p. 270.

12 Deckard's voice-over was removed from both the 1992 'Director's Cut' and the 2007 'Final Cut' versions of the movie.

13 Brian McHale, *Constructing Postmodernism* (London, 1992), p. 147.

14 Curly's story – lest we start to feel too sorry for him – also underlines *Chinatown*'s sober message about the exploitation of women. When Gittes turns up at Curly's house towards the end of the film, his wife answers the door sporting a black eye, presumably after being punished by her husband.

15 Walter Benjamin, 'Little History of Photography', in Michael W. Jennings, Howard Eiland and Gary Smith, eds, *Walter Benjamin: Selected Writings, Part 2: 1931–1934* (Cambridge, MA, 1999), pp. 507–31; p. 527.

16 Incidentally, this episode nearly exemplifies Bonitzer's theory, discussed in chapter Two, of how the suspense thriller creates a labyrinth for the eye by withholding and revealing what is off-screen.

17 Henry Bond, *Lacan at the Scene* (London and Cambridge, MA, 2009), p. 175.

18 Joan Copjec, 'The Phenomenal Nonphenomenal: Private Space in *Film Noir*', in Copjec, ed., *Shades of Noir* (London and New York, 1991), pp. 167–97; p. 189.

19 Ibid., p. 178.

20 See, for example, the essays in E. Ann Kaplan, ed., *Women in Film Noir* (London, 1978).

21 Janey Place, 'Women in Film Noir', in Kaplan, ed., *Women in Film Noir*, pp. 35–67; pp. 44–5.

22 Mulvey, 'Visual Pleasure and Narrative Cinema', p. 272.

23 Arthur Conan Doyle, 'A Case of Identity' [1891], in *The Adventures and Memoirs of Sherlock Holmes* (London, 2001), p. 27. The term 'detective' is derived from the Latin *dētegere*, to uncover, discover, and reveal (*OED*), though it has been suggested that the term carries the connotations of 'unroofing' (because 'tegere' comes from the French

for 'thatch'), 'unroof'. See Andrea Trodd, *Domestic Crime in the Victorian Novel* (Basingstoke, 1989); and Kirsten Moana Thompson, *Crime Films: Investigating the Scene* (London and New York, 2007), p. 33.

24 Christopher Nolan, *Following* (screenplay), in *Memento and Following* (London, 2001), pp. 2–89; p. 26.

25 Sigmund Freud, 'The "Uncanny"' [1919], in *Sigmund Freud*, vol. 14: *Art and Literature* (Harmondsworth, 1990), pp. 335–76; p. 347.

26 Christine Gledhill, '*Klute* 2: Feminism and *Klute*', in Kaplan, ed., *Women in Film Noir*, pp. 112–18; p. 127.

27 Ibid., p. 119.

28 Slavoj Žižek, *The Metastases of Enjoyment: Six Essays on Women and Causality* (London and New York, 1994), pp. 120–21.

29 Peter Shaffer, *The Private Ear / The Public Eye: Two Plays* (London, 1964).

30 Porter, *The Pursuit of Crime*, pp. 122–5.

31 Messent, 'Introduction', p. 8.

32 Ibid., p. 10.

33 Gledhill, '*Klute* 2', p. 116.

Conclusion

1 Peter Messent, 'Introduction: From Private Eye to Police Procedural – The Logic of Contemporary Crime Fiction', in Messent, ed., *Criminal Proceedings: The Contemporary American Crime Novel* (London and Chicago, IL, 1997), pp. 1–21; p. 10.

2 This flimsy boundary is explored at greater length in Bran Nicol, *Stalking* (London, 2006).

3 Ian Burrell and Mark Olden, 'Exposed after eight years: a private eye's dirty work for Fleet Street', *Independent* (14 September 2011); Nick Davies and Amelia Hill, 'Missing Milly Dowler's voicemail was hacked by News of the World', *The Guardian* (5 July 2011); James Cusick and Cahal Milmo, 'NOTW hired disgraced private investigator to protect fake Sheikh', *The Independent* (12 December 2011); Cusick and Milmo, 'Phone hacking: victims' lawyers were targeted', *The Independent* (3 September 2011).

4 Cited in John T. Irwin, *Unless the Threat of Death is Behind Them: Hard-Boiled Fiction and Film Noir* (Baltimore, MD, 2006), p. 45.

Bibliography

Athanasourelis, John Paul, *Raymond Chandler's Philip Marlowe:
    The Hard-Boiled Detective Transformed* (Jefferson, NC, 2012)
Auster, Paul, *City of Glass*, in *The New York Trilogy* (London, 1987)
Bachelard, Gaston, *The Poetics of Space* [1958] (Boston, MA, 1994)
Bazin, André, 'Theatre and Cinema, Parts 1 and 2' [1951], *What is
    Cinema?* [1967], trans. by Hugh Gray (Berkeley and Los Angeles,
    CA, 2005)
Benjamin, Walter, 'On Some Motifs in Baudelaire', *Illuminations*,
    trans. Harry Zohn (New York, 1969), pp. 155—200
——, *Charles Baudelaire: A Lyric Poet in the Era of High Capitalism*,
    trans. Harry Zohn (London and New York, 1983)
——, 'Little History of Photography', in Michael W. Jennings,
    Howard Eiland and Gary Smith, eds, *Walter Benjamin: Selected
    Writings, Part 2: 1931–1934* (Cambridge, MA, 1999), pp. 507–31
Biesen, Sheri Chinen, *Blackout: World War II and the Origins of Film
    Noir* (Baltimore, MD, 2005)
Bond, Henry, *Lacan at the Scene* (London and Cambridge, MA, 2009)
Bonitzer, Pascal, 'Partial Vision: Film and the Labyrinth', *Wide Angle*,
    no. 4 (1981), pp. 56–63
Borde, Raymond and Etienne Chaumeton, 'Towards a Definition of
    Film Noir', extract from *Panorama du Film Noir Américain*, in
    Alain Silver and James Ursini, eds, *Film Noir Reader II* (New
    York, 1996), pp. 17–26
Brevda, William, 'Search for the Originary Sign of Noir: Poe's "Man of
    the Crowd"', *Mythosphere*, II /4 (November 2000), pp. 357–68
Bronfen, Elisabeth, *Home in Hollywood: The Imaginary Geography of
    Cinema* (New York, 2004)

Chandler, Raymond, *The Big Sleep* [1939] (Harmondsworth, 1970)
——, 'The Simple Art of Murder' [1944], in Frank McShane, ed.,
    Chandler: Later Novels and Other Writings (New York, 1995),
    pp. 977–92
Christianson, Scott R., 'Tough Talk and Wisecracks: Language as
    Power in American Detective Fiction', *The Journal of Popular
    Culture*, XXIII/2 (Fall 1989), pp. 151–62
Cook, Pam, 'Duplicity in *Mildred Pierce*', in E. Ann Kaplan, ed.,
    Women in Film Noir (London, 1978), pp. 68–82
Copjec, Joan, ed., *Shades of Noir* (London and New York, 1993)
——, 'The Phenomenal Nonphenomenal: Private Space in *Film
    Noir*', in Joan Copjec, ed., *Shades of Noir* (London and New
    York), pp. 167–97
Damico, James, 'Film Noir: A Modest Proposal', *Film Reader 3*
    (February, 1978), pp. 48–57
Davies, Mike, *City of Quartz: Excavating the Future in Los Angeles*
    (London, 2006)
Eaton, Michael, *Chinatown* (London, 1997)
Erickson, Todd, 'Kill Me Again: Movement Becomes Genre', in Alain
    Silver and James Ursini, eds, *The Film Noir Reader* (New York,
    1996), pp. 307–30
Forter, Greg, *Murdering Masculinities: Fantasies of Gender and Violence
    in the American Crime Novel* (London and New York, 2000)
Foucault, Michel, *Discipline and Punish* (Harmondsworth, 1977)
Frank, Nino, 'A New Kind of Police Drama: The Criminal
    Adventure', in Alain Silver and James Ursini, eds, *Film Noir
    Reader II* (New York, 2004), pp. 15–20
Freud, Sigmund, 'The "Uncanny"' [1919], in *Art and Literature*,
    Penguin Freud Library, XIV (Harmondsworth, 1990), pp. 335–76
Frye, Northrop, *Anatomy of Criticism: Four Essays* [1957] (Princeton,
    NJ, 1971)
——, *The Secular Scripture: A Study of the Structure of Romance*
    (Cambridge, MA, 1957)
Gledhill, Christine, '*Klute* 1: A Contemporary Film Noir and
    Feminist Criticism', in E. Ann Kaplan, ed., *Women in Film Noir*
    (London, 1978), pp. 6–21
——, '*Klute* 2: Feminism and *Klute*', in E. Ann Kaplan, ed., *Women*

in Film Noir (London, 1978), pp. 112–28

Gunning, Tom, *D. W. Griffith and the Origins of American Narrative Film: The Early Years at Biograph* (Chicago, IL, 1994)

——, 'Urban Spectatorship, Poe, Benjamin, and *Traffic in Souls* (1913)', *Wide Angle*, XIX/4 (1997), pp. 25–61

Hammett, Dashiell, *The Maltese Falcon* [1929] (London, 2002)

Harvey, Sylvia, 'Woman's Place: The Absent Family of Film Noir', in E. Ann Kaplan, ed., *Women in Film Noir* (London, 1978), pp. 22–34

Hirsch, Foster, *Detours and Lost Highways: A Map of Neo-Noir* (New York, 1999)

Hirsch, Foster, *The Dark Side of the Screen: Film Noir* (New York, 2001)

Irwin, John, *Unless the Threat of Death is Behind Them: Hard-Boiled Fiction and Film Noir* (Baltimore, MD, 2006)

Jameson, Fredric, 'Cognitive Mapping', in Cary Nelson and Lawrence Grossberg, eds, *Marxism and the Interpretation of Culture* (Chicago, IL, 1987), pp. 347–60

——, 'Postmodernism and Consumer Society'. In Hal Foster, ed., *The Anti-Aesthetic: Essays on Post-Modern Culture* (Seattle, 1989), pp. 111–25

——, *Postmodernism, or the Cultural Logic of Late Capitalism* (London and New York, 1991)

——, 'The Synoptic Chandler', in Joan Copjec, ed., *Shades of Noir* (London and New York, 1993), pp. 33–56

——, *Archaeologies of the Future: The Desire Called Utopia and Other Science Fictions* (London and New York, 2005)

Kaplan, E. Ann, ed., *Women in Film Noir* (London, 1978)

Krutnik, Frank, *In a Lonely Street: Film Noir, Genre, Masculinity* (London, 1991)

MacCannell, Dean, 'Democracy's Turn: On Homeless Noir', in Jean Copjec, ed., *Shades of Noir* (London and New York, 1991), pp. 279–98

Marcus, Steven, 'Introduction to *The Continental Op*' [1974], in Glenn W. Most and William W. Stowe, eds, *The Poetics of Murder: Detective Fiction and Literary Theory* (San Diego, CA, 1983), pp. 197–209

Marling, William, *Raymond Chandler* (Woodbridge, CT, 1986)
——, *The American Roman Noir: Hammett, Cain, and Chandler*
(Athens, GA, and London, 1995)
Mayer, Geoff and Brian McDonnell, *Encyclopaedia of Film Noir*
(Westport, CT, 2007)
McHale, Brian, 'The (Post)Modernism of *The Name of the Rose*',
in *Constructing Postmodernism* (London, 1992), pp. 145–64
Merivale, Patricia, 'Gumshoe Gothics: Poe's "The Man of the
Crowd" and his Followers', in Patricia Merivale and Susan
Elizabeth Sweeney, *Detecting Texts: The Metaphysical Detective
Story from Poe to Postmodernism* (Philadelphia. PA, 1999),
pp. 101–16
Messent, Peter, 'Introduction: From Private Eye to Police Procedural
– The Logic of Contemporary Crime Fiction', in Messent, ed.,
Criminal Proceedings: The Contemporary American Crime Novel
(London and Chicago, IL, 1997), pp. 1–21
Miller, D. A., *The Novel and the Police* (Berkeley and Los Angeles, CA,
and London, 1989)
Mizejewski, Linda, *Hard Boiled and High Heeled: The Woman
Detective in Popular Culture* (London and New York, 2004)
Moretti, Franco, 'Clues', in *Signs Taken for Wonders* (London and
New York, 1984), pp. 130–56
Mulvey, Laura, 'Visual Pleasure and Narrative Cinema' [1975],
in Lizbeth Goodman, ed., *Routledge Reader in Gender and
Performance* (London, 1998), pp. 270–75
Naremore, James, *More Than Night: Film Noir in its Contexts*
(Berkeley and Los Angeles, CA, 1998)
Nolan, Christopher, *Following* [screenplay], in *Memento and
Following* (London, 2001), pp. 2–89
Poe, Edgar Allan, 'The Man of the Crowd' [1840], *The Fall of the
House of Usher, and Other Writings* (Harmondsworth, 1986),
pp. 179–88
Porter, Dennis, *The Pursuit of Crime: Art and Ideology in Detective
Fiction* (New Haven, CT, 1981)
Pynchon, Thomas, *The Crying of Lot 49* [1965] (London, 2007)
Rafferty, Terrence, 'A Gumshoe Adrift, Lost in the '70s [On Altman's
The Long Goodbye]', *The New York Times*, 15 April 2007:

http://www.nytimes.com/2007/04/15/movies/15raff.html

Ross, Kristin, 'Watching the Detectives', in Niall Lucy, ed., *Postmodern Literary Theory: An Anthology* (Oxford, 2000), pp. 197–217

Rossell, Deoc, *Living Pictures: The Origins of the Movies* (Albany, NY, 1998)

Roth, Marty, *Foul and Fair Play: Reading Genre in Classic Detective Fiction* (Athens, GA, 1995)

Rubin, Martin, *Thrillers* (Cambridge, 1999)

Schatz, Thomas, *Hollywood Genres: Formulas, Film-making, and the Studio System* (New York, 1981)

Schrader, Paul, 'Notes on Film Noir', in Barry Keith Grant, *Film Genre Reader III, Volume 3* (Austin, TX, 2003), pp. 229–42

Shaffer, Peter, *The Private Ear / The Public Eye: Two Plays* (London, 1964)

Sobchack, Vivian, 'Lounge Time: Postwar Crises and the Chronotope of Film Noir', in Nick Browne, ed., *Refiguring American Film Genres: History and Theory* (Berkeley, CA, 1998), pp. 129–70

Spicer, Andrew, *Film Noir* (Harlow, 2002)

Telotte, J. P., *Voices in the Dark: The Narrative Patterns of Film Noir* (Chicago, 1989)

Todorov, Tzvetan, 'The Typology of Detective Fiction', in *The Poetics of Prose*, trans. Richard Howard (New York, 1977), pp. 42–52

Tuska, John, *Dark Cinema: American Film Noir in Cultural Perspective* (Westport, CT, 1984)

Vernet, Marc, 'Film Noir on the Edge of Doom', in Joan Copjec, ed., *Shades of Noir* (London and New York, 1993), pp. 1–32

Werner, James V., *American Flaneur: The Cosmic Physiognomy of Edgar Allan Poe* (London, 2004)

Žižek, Slavoj, *Looking Awry: An Introduction to Jacques Lacan through Popular Culture* (Cambridge, MA, 1991)

——, *The Metastases of Enjoyment: Six Essays on Women and Causality* (London and New York, 1994)

——, *Enjoy Your Symptom! Jacques Lacan in Hollywood and Out* (2nd edn, London, 2001)

Ackowledgements

I would like to thank Michael Leaman at Reaktion Books for the invitation to write a book for the Locations series, and Vivian Constantin-opoulos and the team at Reaktion for their help and patience. The Faculty of Arts and Social Sciences at the University of Portsmouth provided financial support to give papers on crime fiction and film at conferences and to relieve some of my teaching load. Researching and writing this book spanned four homes, three towns and two jobs. It is perhaps not surprising that I began to see in films about the private eye, that fearless, nomadic, 'lone wolf', a subtle but unmistakeable yearning for stability. Thankfully I had my perfect companion to guide me through. This book is dedicated to her.

Index

Numerals in italics refer to pages with illustrations